WAREHOUSES

Text **Ann De Kelver** Photography **Koen Van Damme**

WAREHOUSES
Witnesses of prosperity

lannoo

Preface	**The customer finally on top?**
Introduction	**Warehouses in the spotlight**
1	**Warehouses alive!**
2	**Back to basics**
3	**Warehouses have the goods**
4	**Mastering the economic 'blur'**
5	**Warehouses, managing time, space and value**
6	**Let the market in…**
7	**A simply better future**

The customer finally on top?

Most of our cities started as storage depots. Thus, it was no accident that in the medieval city of Ieper, the Clothmakers' Hall was built first – as a storage depot for the weavers – and later the proud Belfry. It was only after the weavers had enough wool to constantly meet the fluctuating demand – and not sooner – that the city could really begin to grow. The development of Nieuwpoort, as the sea harbour of Ieper, was also stimulated by this.

When the economic centre of gravity in the Low Countries shifted from Bruges to Antwerp at the end of the fifteenth century, this was also related to the warehouses. Emperor Maximilian of Austria could think of no greater punishment for rebellious Bruges than to force the Hanse Merchants to move their warehouses to Antwerp. This loss was much harder on the Bruges economy than the silting-up of the Zwin. Thanks to those warehouses, Antwerp could begin its development as a world harbour.

The first warehouse annex-cities developed of course on valuable traffic arteries. They were usually a distance of about 40 kilometres apart, which was a day's journey with a horse and cart. Centuries later, when the first cities developed in the hinterlands of the

United States, the distance between storage depots was a day-trip by train. Thus, warehouses have determined where cities developed.

The next challenge was to effectively defend the temporary stocks in the warehouses from plunderers. Later in this book you will read how the London Docks, which accommodated treasures from the whole world, were protected by walls that were nine metres high. Fortunately, in the meantime, the danger has decreased that gangs of robbers, or jealous neighbouring cities, would come and plunder the depots. In the seventies of the last century, the citizens were even so civilised that they could freely walk around in the 'warehouses'. As a result, 'choice crazy' consumers are now making endless demands on modern warehouses and logistics.
With 40,000 different products in each supermarket (read chapter 3), the current warehouse is threatened from within: it staggers under the weight of the whims of the exacting customer. And this 'new threat' has now become so real that an expert such as the American professor, Barry Schwartz, author of *The Paradox of Choice: Why More is Less*, pleads for a limitation of the choice of the consumer.

It is no wonder that suppliers of fast-moving consumer goods are being gradually forced to reorganise and/or simplify their assortment. The pressure on warehousing is such that manufacturers and distributors in this world are slashing their assortment that is out of hand. Not too long ago, Unilever deleted 800 items. Also clothing shops, where until recently the customer got indigestion from the over-full racks – choosing was a chore, shopping was an ordeal, and buying an exception – have now made a slimmed-down preselection for you.

For the warehouses, this new trend toward less choice, categorisation and/or exclusivity is providing – just in time? – a little more breathing space. With this excellent book, author Ann De Kelver and photographer Koen Van Damme have proven that the curtain has not yet gone down on the vital role of warehouses in our economic life.

Nathalie Bekx *Trend research bureau Bekx&X*

WAREHOUSES IN THE SPOTLIGHTS

Warehouses are not real eye-catchers. They have little aura about them, are not very lavish, are far from being crowd-pullers. They remain so unassuming in the background that we do not realise how important they are to society.

Warehouses not only provide us with everything we need, they anticipate what we will want. They help to determine our standard of living. And it has never been higher. We are no longer docile sheep, we have become demanding wolves. We do not only buy what we need. We buy what we personally find to be nice, trendy, striking and original, or simply, because we enjoy buying things. We evaluate, and make or break a product. We are the merciless judges who direct the consumer society. Warehouses are the unobtrusive links between people and their goods. They are part of the answer to the demand of the customer that might peak today and disappear tomorrow. They try to take advantage of the ascendance of the consumer and are driven by the market, a market that is lubricated by information, because the information economy has driven the efficiency of the market to the top. Everything, both in daily and in business life, works in 'real time'. Everyone, people, companies, countries, even products, are electronically connected with something or someone. The value of the intangible, of the immaterial was never so great.

This flood of information frustrates our traditional certainties and references.

Taking advantage of the market, leading on the basis of continually new, often still unknown rules, is only possible by opening up the boundaries of your company to the market, by welcoming the market into your company. Warehouses that respect the rules of the market and know how to take advantage of them, are much more than ingenious 'state-of-the-art warehouses' that the competition might imitate or even improve. They are logistic 'total concepts' the value of which exceeds by far the material value of the building. They are the creation of the market, which can only be interpreted by the 'real estate specialist'.

This book is not about the technical architectural aspects of logistic buildings. Nor is it about order-picking systems, warehouse lay-out or internal transport systems. It is a book, easy for all to understand, that via warehouses confronts us with how we live. It places warehouses in the spotlight of society because warehouses provide us with everything we need. They are probably older than our written history. They are our treasure houses, past and present.

WAREHOUSES ALIVE!

What path have our goods followed before they reached their destination? The thick woollen coat for the winter months? The inexpensive colourful T-shirt? The fragrant coffee of a well-known brand? The porcelain cup in which that coffee tastes so much better? The exotic fish, as fresh as if it had just been caught? The banana, not too mealy, not too green? The green beans, crisp and fresh, even in the middle of the winter?

And the expensive clock, gold, diamonds or weapons, all goods that can only be transported and stored under continual surveillance? Or, toxic substances and explosives that must be handled with the greatest care? They all seem to find their way automatically and without difficulty to the customer. They are always there, when and where we need them. Even in very large cities of more than 10 million population, the stock seems to be inexhaustible and always up to date.

How is it possible that day after day the most diverse wishes and needs of millions of people in the whole world are taken care of? Ingenious logistic systems are providing consumers with goods and services as efficiently and effectively as possible.

Briefly stated, logistics is the management of the goods flow in the whole chain, beginning at the source of the raw materials and ending where the final products are used. Each important step in the 'supply chain' – the movement of goods from the manufacturer to the user – requires space for the storage and distribution of goods. The same way that a high water-level in a river facilitates boat passage, stocks facilitate the smooth flow of the various steps of the industrial process. Stocks disconnect the import, transit and export times of the sequential operations from each other. Operations become less dependent on each other, which makes the production process more flexible.

Management of the flow of goods is not a simple task. Modern infrastructure, modern modes of transport and communication, and the liberalisation of trade have made us into 'global consumers'. Each day we use products that are made of parts or raw materials originating from the far corners of the globe. Logistic chains are continually becoming longer and their management is becoming more complex.

Stock management has also become a separate profession. Take the simple example of fuel for our automobiles. Without thinking about it, we just assume that a supply will always be present and that it will be available anywhere. Should we tank up today or wait till tomorrow, now or would it be better go several kilometres farther? For us it is the most common thing in the world to have these choices. And we know exactly why we make each choice. With a quick keystroke we compare price, quality, delivery conditions, availability, etc.

For traditional products – goods that do not spoil or become out-of-date because of innovation – maintaining a certain amount of stock still seems feasible. But how should we deal with 'time sensitive goods' such as food stuffs or high-technology products? Someone who lays in a stock of digital cameras today might discover tomorrow that the stock has become absolutely worthless because a Japanese, American or European manufacturer has brought a new model onto the market with a much higher resolution and with all kinds of interesting software included. He will no longer be able to sell his out-of-date model to a clever customer, who already knows about the trendy features of the new model.

Maintaining stocks involves risks and costs money. First, the stock itself is inactive money. An investment must also be made in space for storing the goods. And finally, the stored goods run the risk of damage, spoilage or obsolescence (against which one is able to obtain insurance, but that of course also costs money). The trick is to keep the right stock on hand. The right quantity, at the right place and in the right circumstances. Especially in recent years, companies have become very conscious of this.

Whereas in the past companies were able to entice their customers with traditional advantages such as the quality of their products, their productivity, their technical innovation or their marketing, they have now discovered logistics. In the whole chain, with its costs for transport, storage, goods handling, communication and administration, great competitive advantages can be realised, which can be decisive.

The now widely-known JIT system from the early eighties of the previous century is a typical example of rationalisation of stocks. The idea comes from Japan where maintaining stocks is very expensive because of the prohibitive price of land. According to this logistic concept, no stock is held, or only an absolute minimum. Goods are delivered just in time to be immediately incorporated into the production process. The most successful application of JIT is probably the 'Kanban system', developed by the Japanese automobile manufacturer, Toyota. 'Kanbans' (Japanese for cards) are information carriers that transmit

information upstream, in other words, from the consumer to the manufacturer, throughout the production process. The 'Kanbans' pull the products through the production chain (pull system) at the rhythm of the consumer.

↑ *Certainly for perishables, it is an art to maintain availability of the right amount, at the right place and under the right conditions.*

Having the whole production smoothly driven by the market is certainly not possible for all products. It requires a frequent and regularly recurring demand and a repetitive production plan, in brief, as few surprises as possible. In addition, stocks can only be decreased in a production process with a very balanced, advanced and thus expensive production apparatus for which timing is crucial, because every delay, a missed flight, traffic congestion, a delay in shipping because of bad weather, has a domino-effect that could have been avoided by having the right stock. And, this risk could turn out to be very expensive for the manufacturer, much more expensive than the price of a certain level of stock. It might not be possible to supply the ordered product as expected and the company can lose a customer to the competition because the customer cannot or does not want to wait. The market does not tolerate a 'slow response'. More than ever, timing is a critical success factor.

Take Amazon, for example, the 'dot-com retailer' of books. The remarkable international expansion of this company does not result from the quality of the products it offers its customers (they can also be found at other places), nor can it be attributed to the exceptional discounts that it might give on the best-sellers, or the latest electronic gadgets that it offers. Rather, it has everything to do with the logistics. Someone who orders from Amazon will be handed the products at his front door sooner that he expects. The speed and correctness of what is called the 'fulfilment', the execution of an order, results in satisfied and thus faithful customers. This speed and correctness requires an excellent functioning logistic system with a carefully planned stock.

→ *For speed and correctness in fulfilment, a smoothly functioning logistic system is required with an optimal stock for each specific product.*

Logistics, sometimes called derisively 'pushing boxes' in the past, has become a complex discipline. At present the expression certainly holds true: 'Every battle that was ever lost, every battle that was ever won, was lost or won because of logistics'. Until recently, logistic costs made up about 10% of the total cost of products. In the meantime, this percentage has increased substantially. The economy is growing, especially in expensive, technological products where innovation occurs very fast and for which very high logistic requirements must be met. Furthermore, the new consumer is no longer a 'mass consumer'. He wants to obtain exactly the right product at the time and at the place he needs it, for an attractive price, and without any delay. Mass consumption is slowly being replaced by the new phenomenon, 'lean consumption', which places unprecedented requirements on logistic functions.

Traditional warehouses will certainly not disappear. Goods with a low value, low inventory costs or that are less time-sensitive, will always be stored. But in addition the need has arisen for a new kind of warehouse, a warehouse with a design that is a determining factor in the international competitive battle between

companies. These new warehouses serve to a lesser degree as traditional warehouses: they have become 'pass trough centres', service centres that facilitate the speed and the quality of the distribution. They are 'logistic solutions', ingenious 'tailor made' designs that are not only oriented toward distribution and storage but also provide a whole range of other activities. They are 'flex-buildings' that can absorb without difficulty the ceaseless, often turbulent, changes in the sector.

↓ *Each step in the supply chain requires space to store and to distribute the goods.*

BACK
TO BASICS

Warehouses appear to be a child of the twenty-first century, the visible symbol of our modern consumer society. But nothing is less true. Although the size and inventive complexity of modern warehouses are in part a response to our unpredictable, limitless urge to consume, their prototype came into being several thousand years ago.

The first primitive forms of logistics developed as soon as people started organising themselves into groups. The larger these groups became, the more sophisticated their logistic systems had to be, and the more important storage space became as a link in the movement of goods from the manufacturer to the user.

Those warehouses of the past, without the advanced techniques of our current 'logistic platforms', simply and clearly demonstrate what the basic function, the essence, of warehouses was and still is. They are the essential buffers that absorb the imperfections in the flow of goods from the manufacturer to a community of users. They are part of the answer to the needs of groups of people. Those needs have changed and have made warehouses into 'logistic platforms', but the basic function has remained unchanged: storing, in the best possible circumstances, the goods that people need and/or want. They are the treasure houses of the past and of the present.

The remains of earlier storage buildings are the surviving evidence of the affluence of peoples and kingdoms in the past. The ruins of the warehouses of the Roman Empire, dating from the first century, and the London docks from the eighteenth century, are the two most interesting examples of storage facilities that served as true treasure houses.

Several thousand years before Christ, when writing had been invented, mankind had discovered that living together in a group had important advantages. The strongest of the tribe went hunting, the most dextrous made nets to catch fish. Tasks were divided and assigned to 'the best in the field'; a first form of specialisation arose. Things were no longer produced exclusively for one's own use. The boat-maker needed fish to stay alive and the fisherman could catch fish for the whole tribe if he had a boat. A need developed for a first, although very rudimentary, form of logistics. The political leader, the head of the tribe, was the logistics organiser of the group. He saw to it that there were sufficient people specialised in certain tasks and he co-ordinated the distribution of the products and goods among his fellow tribesmen.

Yet, twenty well-organised healthy people can easily be defeated by forty starving (and therefore aggressive) hunters. Although economic efficiency and superiority were extremely important in the development of societies, it was in particular the rise of military might that explains the emergence of large groups and real kingdoms. The rise of whole empires introduced the necessity for more advanced logistic systems with real warehouses. The Roman Empire is an outstanding example. The remains of the immense Roman warehouses are still silent witnesses of their remarkably efficient logistic network (taking into consideration, of course, the possibilities and needs of the time).

→ *The remains of immense storage places are surviving evidence of the prosperity and dominance of the Roman Empire.*

In the last centuries before Christ, the Roman Empire was able year after year to expand its power and enforce its authority until the entire rich Mediterranean area (and even beyond) was in its power. Rome became a superpower, a megalopolis with almost a million people. To meet the needs of its population, and also of its legions, a rigorous, ingenious network had to be implemented to allow Mediterranean riches to flow to Rome and the provinces, to store them, and then to distribute them again. It is difficult to overestimate the importance of the efficiency of the Roman logistic network. People had to eat. Social peace was at stake. Per day and per person, about one kilo of grain was needed, which came mostly from Egypt. 'All roads lead to Rome' could be taken literally at that time because millions of tons of provisions were transported daily from the whole Mediterranean area to Rome and the provinces. The (governmental) logistic network was not only carefully thought-out, it was also very disciplined and was strictly supervised.

Of course the quantity of grain used daily was not identical to the quantity that could be imported each day. For a continual provisioning of all Romans – also during the winter months – stocks, reserves, were needed. Provisions were stored in what were called horrea or warehouses. The larger the size of the stocks in the horrea, the more unperturbed – and thus the more tranquil – the plebeians were, and thus the greater the stability of the dominion. Because of the political importance of the horrea, they were thoroughly worked out conceptually so their valuable contents remained safely stored. To protect food from moisture and all kinds of vermin (insects, rats, mice and birds) the buildings had to be hermetically sealed, they needed a low temperature and dry atmosphere, and little light should be admitted. The dark, oppressive, confining buildings not only ensured an optimal preservation of the provisions, but also made it possible to efficiently control the traffic of people and goods going in and out of the warehouses.

There were various types of storage buildings, but the most prevalent construction model appears to be that of Hortensius (27 BC). The massive-appearing building, with thick walls and only one small entrance, consisted of a large central hall, 62 by 25 metres, where the goods were prepared for storage, surrounded by a gallery and 38 small *cellae*. The *cellae*, each of which had only one narrow entrance of approximately 1.75 metres, were the actual warehouses.

The remains of ancient horrea are a lasting confirmation of the wealth and power of the Roman Empire. Another exceptional example dates from the eighteenth, beginning of the nineteenth century. The harbour of London, surrounded by docks with warehouses, was the incarnation of the greatness and wealth of the British Empire. London was then, literally and figuratively, the warehouse of the world.

40

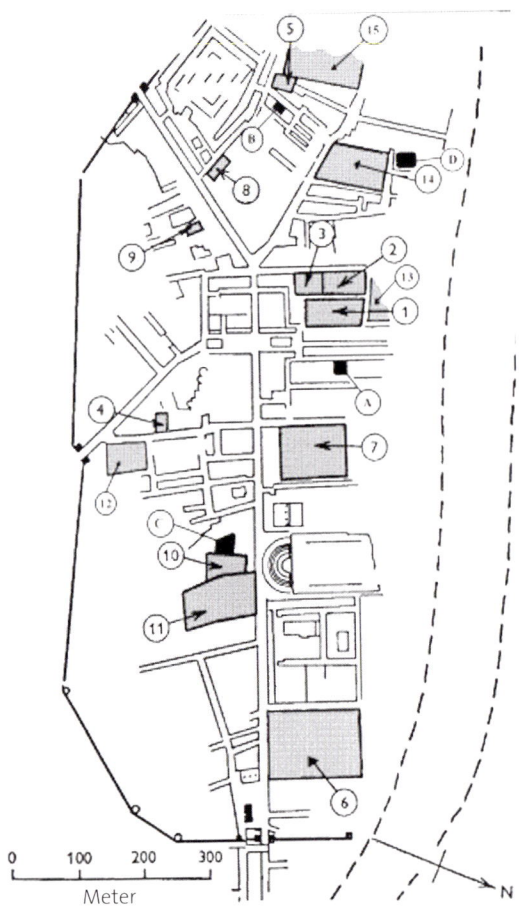

↑ *Overview of the warehouses along the Via Ostia*

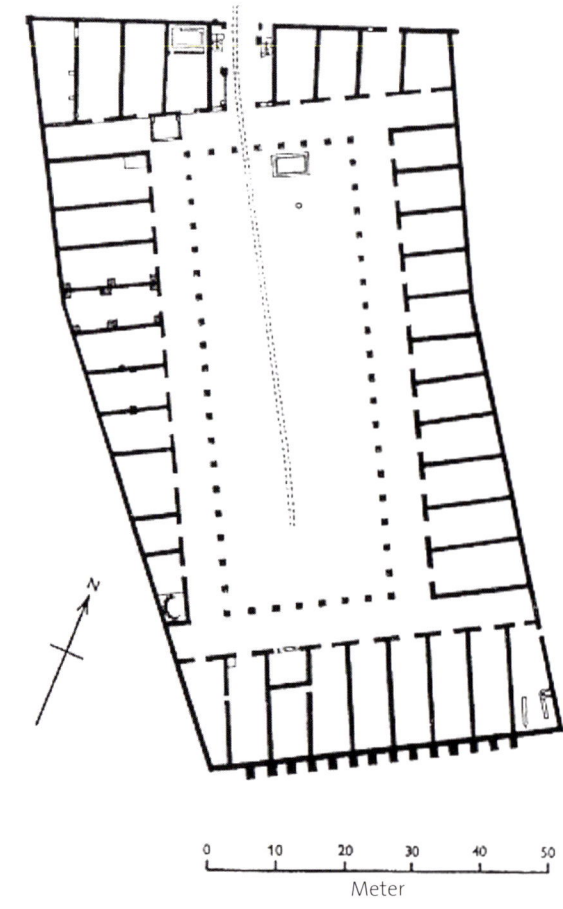

↑ *Overview of the warehouses of Hortensius according to G. Rickman*

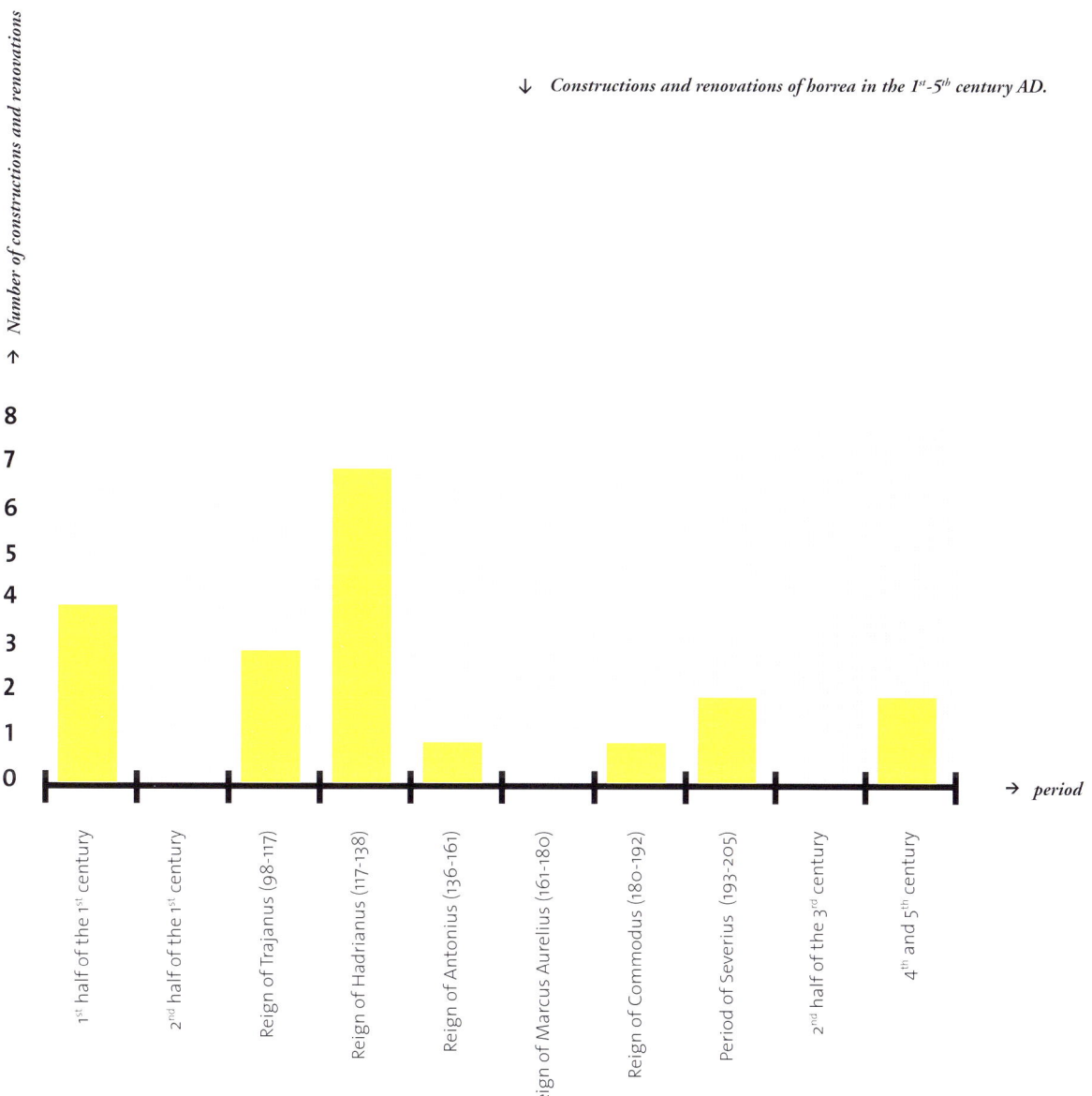

Constructions and renovations of horrea in the 1st-5th century AD.

Since the fall of the Roman Empire, London had become an important harbour. Riches from the whole world were brought by ship and were stored in the harbour to be transported farther to their destination. At the end of the eighteenth century, under the influence of the budding industrial revolution, ship traffic on the Thames became so busy that more than 2000 loaded ships reached the London harbour each day. The capacity of both the commercial wharves and the warehouses for the import of all kinds of goods, such as sugar, tobacco, rice, wine, grain, maize, iron and rubber soon became insufficient for the fast growth of London. Ships sometimes had to wait for weeks someplace on the Thames before they could be unloaded, which blocked access to the harbour. The delays, confusion and attendant criminality, alarmed London. There was an urgent need for modernisation and efficiency.

At the end of the eighteenth century an all-out effort was made to build docks. This system, with which the navy had experimented previously, consisted of gigantic basins with a large constant surface area and a guaranteed draught, in which ships could tie up. The docks were surrounded by immense hangars (for transit goods) and warehouses, so the goods could be stored directly from the hold of the ship. The warehouses were as much as six stories high, 150 metres long and 50 metres wide. Each warehouse had two doors, one for receiving and one for dispatching goods. The docks, where the riches of the world were stored, were secured like forts. The walls and gates were often 9 metres high (such as the St. Katherine docks) and there was continual surveillance and security provided by the respective companies.

The new system of docks produced an enormous logistical improvement. Each day, about 4000 boats could be unloaded at the same time with a speed that was unimaginable a hundred years earlier. Whereas it formerly took from 8 to (in the winter) even 14 days to unload a ship of 350 tons, on the average only 12 hours were still required to unload a ship of 250 tons. London became a teeming, modern world harbour, the population of which increased sevenfold in one century (from 1 million at the beginning of the nineteenth century to more than 7 million at the beginning of the First World War).

The docks gave an undeniable impulse to the industrial revolution and the economic expansion of Great Britain and Western Europe. Since then, the continual renewal of the infrastructure, transport systems, storage techniques, methodology for preparing goods for storage, in brief, the entire logistic revolution that resulted, has laid the foundation for our logistic know-how in the twenty-first century.

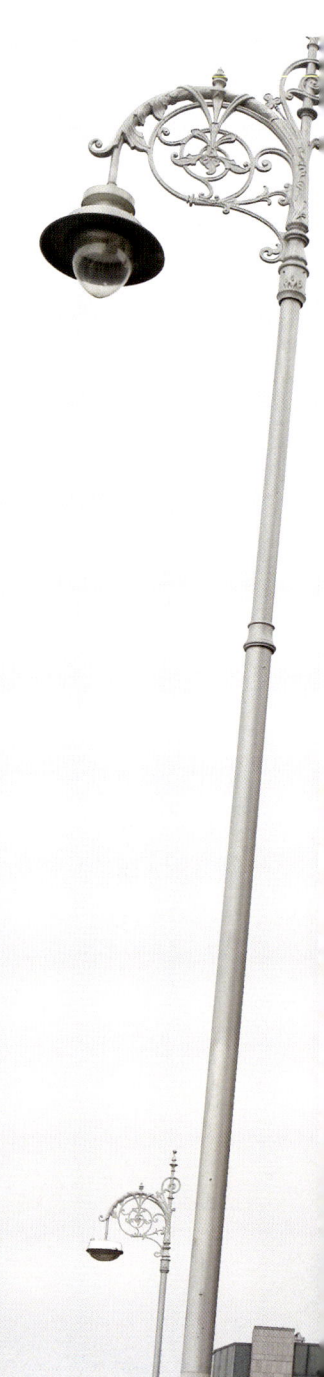

49

52

WAREHOUSES HAVE THE 'GOODS'

That the Romans knew the value of a lavishly filled warehouse is shown by the writings of Tacitus. He describes how the anxious, rebellious plebeians made it difficult for Emperor Claudius in 51 AD because 'there are only 15 days of provisions left in the cellars'. The Romans understood that their warehouses were vital for their welfare, even for their survival.

Although we no longer attribute the same importance to warehouses, they still remain the indispensable links between us and our goods, although we might not realise this. For us the continual presence of that enormous abundance and variety of goods is commonplace. The pen that we write with, the clothing that makes us feel good, the comfortable chair, the apple that we eat as a snack, the water from that attractive bottle, the car that takes us where we want to go, the building we live in… all these things, and/or the parts or raw materials of which they are made, have found their way to us through a warehouse.

Warehouses only show us their importance when something goes wrong, when an urgently needed item can only be delivered after weeks of waiting because it must come from the other side of the world, when a popular item is 'sold out' or 'not in stock'. Warehouses are the unseen links between people and their goods. They are part of the answer to the demand of the customer, that might peak today and disappear tomorrow. They strive to be aware of the often irrational and unpredictable wishes of the customer and to stay one step ahead of them…

In our time warehouses provide us with all those goods that not only determine our well-being, but also our prosperity, our standard of living.

Globalisation, deregulation and digitalisation have catapulted us into a market-crazy world. In our time there are more markets for more things that come from a greater geographic area than ever before. In an American supermarket you can buy as many as 40,000 different products, when you actually only need about 150 to meet most of your needs[1]. Driven by the new technology, the consumer wants everything and preferably immediately. Goods (and of course also money) glide around the world at unprecedented speed. Twenty-four hours of international trade in 2001 was equivalent to the international trade of the whole year in 1949[2]. Whereas we formerly had to be satisfied with 'one-size-fits-all products', we consumers are now running the show. The 'push-economy' has become a 'pull-economy'. Take music, for example. Do you want to hear a song before you buy the CD? Or would you prefer to buy a couple of songs by that performer rather than the whole CD? Do you want to make your own compilation with the songs of that CD, remix them a little and add some bass tones? The old, well-known slogan 'the customer is king' appears to have finally become reality.

The millions of customers who on their own (to a great extent) determine each day which goods they want to have immediately from that enormous variety, present logistic systems with unbelievable challenges.

We have never been more demanding. We subject food stuffs to thorough tests: are they fresh, are they free of artificial colouring, are they low-calorie? Does this item of clothing have the right label? Where was it made? Is that automobile environmentally friendly? Barring a few exceptions, we are not really loyal to brand names. We want the right product, we want the best product, and of course for the most advantageous price. We are called 'smart shoppers'. Some among us are even so 'smart' that they know the products better than the sellers. They are more or less enslaved to the very latest that they have learned about via the newest technologies. They are proactive trend-setters who do not allow anything to be palmed off on them; they determine themselves what is 'hot'; they are called 'prosumers'[3].

We no longer buy only when the shops are open. Via the web we can buy at any moment from anywhere. For some products, we are no longer willing to wait even a moment. For these impulse purchases, a sandwich or a bouquet of flowers at midnight, we can find what we want at the all-night shop or the shop at the petrol station.

We are not always rational in our purchases. Irrational motives make us into very unpredictable shoppers.

The modern shopper does not always buy because he needs something. Who has never bought something impulsively, with that 'got to have it' feeling? At that moment the budget and necessity no longer matter. We do it from emotion, we feel the adrenaline of the perfect purchase, whatever the price might be. You cannot put a price tag on emotion, feeling and experience. According to Nobel Prize winner, Daniel Kahneman, the (so-called rational) individual is willing to drive for twenty minutes to save $20 on a video camera of $200, but he will not walk five blocks to save $40 on a cruise of $2000. Many of our purchases cannot be explained economically or logically, they are not inspired by the quality of a product but by its value to us. And that value is mainly determined by the image that the consumer has of it, and thus to a less extent by the characteristics of the product itself. The range of European brand-name products in Japanese department stores is at least as great as in Europe itself. The quality of these products is of course indisputable, but the Japanese consumer is willing to pay the high(er) price because of the image he has of the goods: exclusive, special, 'in'. An example of products with which consumers have an extremely strong emotional tie are what are called 'love brands'[4]. Why do people still buy a Harley Davidson when a Suzuki, for example, is less expensive, handier, more efficient and more dependable? A 'Harley' is not just a motorcycle, it is a source of emotional satisfaction. That emotional value knows no price..

→ *Many of the things we buy, from a pair of glasses to a camera or computer, free people from limitations in time and space.*

People's purchasing behaviour has been thoroughly studied scientifically. There are complex theories, reference works and real gurus who can explain various aspects of it. But one thing remains certain: our purchasing behaviour remains unpredictable to a great degree. Why does someone carefully compare price and quality today in the supermarket when he buys ingredients for his lunch, and tomorrow he has an extended, luxurious lunch delivered to his house for ten times the price? It often cannot be explained and is even harder to predict. And still, our logistic systems must take it all into account. Each day we expect that at the right moment the desired product will be available and preferably close at hand. In the fashion sector, for example, where goods are 'hot' today and are already 'out' tomorrow, it is not easy to follow the often unpredictable and irrational wishes of the consumer. The Spanish clothing chain, Zara, with its much-talked-about 'super responsive' flow of goods, is exceptionally successful at this. Their clothing can be designed, made, transported and delivered to the enthusiastic customer in their shop in approximately 15 days. This is extremely exceptional in a sector where designers usually plan months in advance what they will place on the market the next season. This 'fast fashion' system of Zara is based on a constant exchange of information with the buyers via all players in the logistic chain, including the designers. But it is accomplished logistically by a carefully worked out capacity in factories and warehouses. The 'fast-response' is made possible by the constant availability of capacity in both the factory and the warehouses. By not using the capacity completely, Zara can react faster than others in the market to unexpected peaks in the demand of its customers.

People buy goods, not only because they need all kinds of things, but also because it makes them feel good. Never before has man spent so much time and energy on buying things, on everything related to our required purchases, both the large and the small. Buying has become an important part of our lives, purchasing is part of our culture. When terrorists demolished the World Trade Center on 11 September 2001, killing thousands of people, and New York City was completely in the doldrums emotionally, Mayor Rudolph Giuliani provided leadership. He told New Yorkers not to go to their work in the vicinity of Wall Street. 'Take a day off... go shopping,' were his words. Mayor Giuliani understood, maybe intuitively, how closely shopping is related to our normal daily lives. He suggested that something quite simple be done, something that could briefly distract New Yorkers and return them to a normal life in spite of everything.

'Civilisations are judged on the basis of the structures they build,' writes Nordström[5]. The Egyptians built the pyramids, the Greeks left us the Acropolis, the Romans, the Coliseum, and the modern age has given us shopping centres. We find 'meaning' in shopping. We can find more petrol stations open 24 hours a day than churches or synagogues. Some call this critically the shallowness of our existence. Each month a book is published somewhere in which the consumer society, and the materialism to which we are supposedly enslaved, are condemned. Do you suppose that these moralising authors only spend their money on worthwhile products after always first expertly evaluating the 'return on investment'? If we all did this, unemployment in the world would be enormous. Since Keynes it has been generally accepted that expenditures, rather than savings, prevent economic depression. Purchasing supplies oxygen to an economy. And conversely, an economy that is doing well attracts shopping centres, luxury boutiques and exclusive products. They are not the symbol of our collective addiction but the proof of our social might and wealth.

The consumer society is actually older than we think. Our obsession for useless, irrational purchases is not a recent cultural phenomenon, it is a primeval biological instinct. Some think that recent archaeological discoveries in Africa and Australia indicate that the production of and trade in jewels and cosmetics already existed 100,000 years ago. According to evolution psychologist Geoffry Miller[6] sexual selection is the driving force behind the explosion of the consumer society: males who are enabled to put energy into superfluous activities, use it to advertise their genetic fitness like a peacock does with his tail. Thus we are 'arch consumers'. Human nature has created the modern world to its own liking. Our so-called 'materialism' may then also not be called an 'outgrowth' but rather 'the cornerstone' of our modern civilisation.

→ *Packaging is certainly important. Before people pair off they often decorate themselves with designer clothes, they buy their feathers. From an evolutionary perspective this is not just vanity, it is characteristic of our human nature.*

MASTERING THE ECONOMIC 'BLUR'

An excess of markets, continually more products, optimum stocks, inexpensive, universally accessible information... the market has become a paradise for the buyer. It is no longer the stock that determines what will be consumed, but the (whimsical) consumer who determines what the stock will be. Logistic systems try to take optimal advantage of the ascendance of the consumer and are market driven.

But there is no 'status-quo' on this market. To the contrary, the market changes continually and the changes occur faster and faster. Each update of the changes would be immediately out-of-date. Any logical subdivision of the changes is random because they are reciprocally each others cause and effect. The most conspicuous silver thread running through the changes is the observation that the information economy is driven by three important forces: speed, connectivity and immaterial value. These forces cause our familiar traditional boundaries to become blurred and even to fade away, both in our daily and in our business lives. Dealing with these forces is often a journey into the unknown.

Companies that want to master this economic 'blur' will have to position themselves around these three forces. Their logistic organisation will play a crucial role in this. In this dynamic context, companies that apply logistic systems designed for a stable environment, need to think again. Flexibility – as a shock absorber for the turbulence – and professionalism – as a reaction to the complexity – will be important core concepts in finding the right answers to the complicated economical work environment. The same core concepts will determine whether a warehouse will meet the requirements of the 'economic blur'.

Our changing perception of space, time, and mass

'We shape our technology and afterwards our technologies shape our way of thinking'[7]. New technology changes, and radically influences, our way of thinking, our habits, our expectations… our whole life. Our existing rules and boundaries become blurred, our way of living is redefined. Technology even succeeds at changing our image of the three most fundamental dimensions of the universe: space, time and mass.

Until recently, physical distance determined the limits of our reach. At present, the whole world is within our reach. Via computer, TV and telephone our connection with each other is unlimited. A digital traffic system, composed of cables and satellites around our earth, enables everyone to receive thousands of interactive channels. Everything, everyone, people, companies, countries (and soon even goods) are connected with each other virtually. We experience a completely new dimension of space.

Instantaneous, unlimited communication has also changed our perception of time. Now that everything can happen fast, we have the feeling that everything must happen fast. Time appears to have become our most precious commodity, our greatest luxury. Time, that we have or do not have, controls our lives. We no longer base our concept of time and our requirements for speed on the rhythm of the clock, but on our experience of what is the fastest possible. If it is possible, then it must be done. In the period before 'Fedex' it was seldom absolutely necessary for something to be at its destination in one night. Now it is always necessary. Formerly we were concerned about the time value of money, now we are more concerned about the value (expressed in money) of time.

The value of goods and services is no longer mainly determined by its material, but by its immaterial characteristics. These immaterial characteristics appear in the form of innovation, the brand name, the licence, the relations, the service, etc. This makes one product more desirable than another, distinguishes one product from all the others. This is why they are not precisely the same products. Starbucks does not just pour coffee, Starbucks pours you your own personalised coffee drink. Singapore Airlines does not just provide you with transportation, your flight is like bathing in the luxury of a five-star hotel. Our economy is becoming increasingly more weightless. Take the PC on your desk. In 1984 hardware was 80% of the cost and software 20% of the total. Now the ratio is exactly the opposite[8].

Traditional boundaries become blurred and disappear, both in our daily and in our business lives. Services and goods are becoming one. The distinction between possession and use is becoming blurred. Buyers are becoming sellers and sellers, buyers. Now houses are also offices and in offices there is a homey atmosphere. That which is real is given a virtual dimension and conversely. Clearly structured 'value chains' become complex economic webs. On all fronts, contradictions melt together into what the futurist Stan Davis calls 'the blur'[9], something vague. It will be our task as consumers, as entrepreneurs, as managers, as people, to recognise the blur, to have a command of its new ground rules, to be able to think outside the box and to have unlimited flexibility.

→ *We no longer base our concept of time and our requirements of speed on the rhythm of the clock, but on our experience of what is the fastest possible.*

The basic drivers of the information economy: speed, connectivity and intangibles

Inexpensive, abundant, universally accessible information is for the market what oil is for a machine. It lubricates the market mechanism and allows the motor to perform better. The more information there is, the more efficiently the market is organised, the less acceptable boundaries become, boundaries in space, boundaries in time, and boundaries between the material and the immaterial aspects of products.

Everything in the company changes and works in 'real time'. Everything is electronically connected with something or someone: products, companies, countries. Each product, each service has both material and immaterial value. Time, space and mass, translated into speed, connectivity and immaterial value, are currently the most important driving forces in the information economy.

→ *Transport infrastructure is an important link in the oneness of the world market.*

A.

THE WORLD-WIDE MARKET: CONNECTIVITY

Modern information technology, the renewal of transport and communication infrastructure, and the increasing liberalisation and homogenisation of governmental policy have led to an increasing internationalisation of trade, and thus to virtually limitless entrepreneurship. In virtually every business sector, the competition extends beyond borders. Transport costs form an increasingly lower threshold. Shipping granite to Aberdeen, Scotland, (also called 'Granite City') would have been dismissed as a big joke previously. Now it is deadly serious. When the city recently restored several buildings, no local stone was used, but stone was imported from China more than 10,000 km away because it was cheaper. The transport costs for sending a ton of goods have decreased by 70% during the last 40 years[10].

The chess game to win national markets has become a wild dance to win the world. Companies have obtained the freedom of movement to restructure themselves geographically and to select with great freedom the optimum method of operation. Activities are disconnected from the traditional sales-market and source locations and are reoriented to the place on the map where they can be carried out most economically.

Originally, geographically distributed activities and departments were solidly bound to each other (centralisation or vertical integration) and gigantic multinationals came into being. This strategy of keeping everything is one's own company worked perfectly as long as information was scarce. But in the meantime the world has changed, there are new ground rules, the market is governed by information because there is an abundance of information. Virtually all activities or parts that one formerly made himself, can now be purchased someplace else more easily. Companies decide to invest their scarce resources only in things at which they are the best, namely in their core competences. They turn the transnational hyper-efficient markets to their advantage, whether it has to do with activities, processes, components, people or parts, and form dynamic joint ventures. All kinds of formal and informal temporary alliances, virtual networks and 'business webs' are increasingly doing the work that a large company formerly did itself. Even routine tasks are increasingly entrusted to specialised companies. Nike and Cisco have outsourced almost their complete production to subcontractors. The textile chain H&M has about 900 suppliers in Europe and Asia. The largest company in the US is no longer GM or IBM, but is the employment agency, ManPower, which in 2002 'employed' almost two million people.

→ *Companies make decisions from a global perspective. Activities are repositioned to the place on the world map where they can be performed most efficiently.*

The challenges presented by the new information society, transform the players on the market. Companies focus on knowing, doing and possessing things that are of unique value, that are world class for a specific group of customers. They prefer to do one thing excellently than many things ordinarily. To do that one unique thing, they only call on the very best teammates. Successful model-companies are becoming more and more network arrangers. They possess a unique concept and utilise the transactional imperfections in the market to do it better and different than anyone else. The network arrangers have introduced to the market the power of a product that exists by collaborating only with the strongest[11].

Geographically distributed co-operating entities can only function as an optimal network, however, if they are connected with each other. Flows of goods,

information and resources are the lifeblood of the network company. To get these flows moving, an infrastructure is needed and a suitable logistic partner. The decentralisation of companies into flexible networks over the whole world has led to a reorganisation of logistics.

↓ *The logistics partner orchestrates the goods flow of a company to obtain an optimally functioning network.*

'If you can't beat them, join them' has also become the motto here. The manufacturers have also become buyers (of logistics). Synergy or centralisation is out-of-date and has been replaced by 'outsourcing'. Welding has been replaced by Velcro, which can provide companies with the strategic flexibility needed for the future. And this certainly applies no less for the logistic functions of a company. Logistics outsourcing is considered to be a very important strategic instrument for gaining competitive advantages.

In the past, physical distribution was probably one of the first tasks that a company would contract out to a professional transport company ('one party logistics' or 1PL). At present, companies call on professional logistics operators for virtually all physical activities in the logistic chain (2PL). Because of the scale advantages and the centralisation of specialised know-how by the logistics operator, logistics 'outsourcing' (usually) means both a cost savings and a quality improvement for companies. In the EU 94% of transport, 65% of distribution and 48% of 'warehouse operations' are contracted out to the 'logistics service provider'[12]. Of the total amount that companies spend on logistics, 61% in Western Europe and 44% in the US is contracted out[13]. The activities that are contracted out the most are 'warehousing' and 'outbound transport' (transport of the outgoing flow of goods) but also customs processing, 'cross-docking' and consolidation (see infra), 'inbound transport' (the transport of the incoming stream of goods), financial services and expedition (express transport) are very often entrusted to logistics service providers.

→ *In the EU 48% of warehouse operations are already outsourced to a logistics service provider.*

Of course, companies prefer to associate themselves with one logistics partner world-wide, the so-called 'one-stop shopping principle'. The service providers adapt themselves for this and, by means of acquisitions and all kinds of joint ventures and alliances, they organise themselves to the extent possible as international operators so they can offer a world-wide service in their specific niche market.

The more that logistic tasks are contracted out to various specialised logistic parties, the more difficult it becomes for a company to see the whole picture (often world-wide) and to co-ordinate 'logistics' as an entity and integrate them into an efficient and effective logistic network. Companies need a 'network arranger', someone who knows logistics through and through, a kind of 'super-manager' who co-ordinates

and supervises all aspects of the logistic chain and who is the sole contact for both the company and the logistics service providers. This service, also called 3PL (sometimes 4PL) or 'contract logistics', has developed during the last decade into a 100 billion industry that is playing an increasingly important role in the economy. In the European Union, where approximately 20% of world logistics occur, 'third-party logistics' are used for approximately one third of the total volume of shipped goods[14]. This is expected to increase. In the US only 38% of the 'Fortune 500-manufacturers' (large American companies) made use of 3PL services in 1991 whereas in 2003 this was no less than 80%[15].

World-wide networks incorporating various logistics service providers and new distribution structures are especially complex. The activities at the various intersections of the distribution structure and the logistics partners and sales organisations that are associated with them must be able to connect with each other seamlessly. Information is needed continuously about where the goods are located in the distribution network. Excellent distribution management and supporting integrated information technology are critical factors for this.

In the same way that the now familiar GPS system in cars continually tracks your position on the road by what is called 'Radio Frequency Identification' technology, goods can be followed throughout the whole 'supply chain' (from the production process to the user) and information can be transmitted. Special labels on the goods (called 'tags'), provided with a chip and a mini-antenna, contain all kinds of information (product number, manufacturer, price, ingredients, etc.) and can be read from a distance without physical contact. This technology, that is still in its infancy at present (and is expensive), is precisely the missing link for which many manufacturers have been waiting. This technology can enable them to keep a minimum of stock without running out, and to optimise the use of their production and distribution capacity[16].

B.

The 'real-time' world market: speed and intangibles

Send a message to the other side of the world and several seconds later the addressee has received it. Order a laptop today and with a little luck you can be using it tomorrow. In Tokyo you can drive around on Friday with your 'customised' Toyota that you ordered on Monday. Via a world-wide electronic network, 41 billion dollars per minute hurtle round the world. The economy runs round the clock. There are no days, no nights. A continual availability, a continual service, is expected day and night.

The speed of the economy changes the meaning of capital and consumer goods. Capital goods were traditionally the durable goods, whereas consumer goods were perishable. But here too the boundaries have become blurred and the distinction more subtle. The speed at which the economy rages forward has also given the (accounting) concept of 'durability' a different meaning.

The machines that were used for production last year are now obsolete and are worth little more than a loaf of last year's bread. The material assets (the capital goods) that were formerly the valuable core of a company, simply because of their durability, have lost their value significantly. A company is no longer evaluated on the basis of its 'assets' or income. For valuation, Wall Street focuses on the immaterial 'growth potential'. Traditional capital goods are behaving more and more like consumer goods. Companies are becoming conscious of this and now want to get their original capital goods in motion and provide them with a 'living value'. They increasingly 'use' their capital goods the same way consumer goods are used. The best known example is, of course, the company that sells its immobile goods and then rents them back so they can invest the 'proceeds' in its core competences. The 'outsourcing' of real estate is no longer a way for companies to scrape together their very last resources. It has become a complicated financial technique with various possibilities, which is applied by the best performing world players (Sony, for example) to increase their competitive strength.

But the lifespan of consumer goods also becomes shorter every day. That which is 'in' today, is already obsolete tomorrow. We choose from many more kinds of products and it is continually easier to persuade us to try different and new products.

Entrepreneurs understand that a fast, and preferably first, penetration of a sales market gives a clear competitive advantage. But speed is not the one-and-only competitive factor: dependability ('reliability') is a second crucial element that is important for logistics service. Companies operate in a market environment that is 'based on time'. This explains the explosive growth of international express companies, which have quickly earned a solid position in world-wide logistics. These express companies deliver approximately 2 million international deliveries per day, with the largest integrator in the US delivering approximately 3.5 billion shipments per year[17].

The classic segmentation of consumers into target groups is increasingly becoming more difficult because of the enormous number of new products that must be delivered to the right customer as fast and as reliably as possible. Whereas mass production occupied a commanding position in the past, 'mass customisation' or 'mass production in the size of the customer' has now become the overriding trend. A generic product is sent as far as possible in mass through the logistic chain. Only at the very end, as close to the customer as possible, the product is 'customised' or made customer-specific. This more or less personalised customer-service development, that relates both to the end-product and to the after-sale and fulfilment service, increases the customer's specifications, the stock rotation and the flexibility needed to anticipate the wishes of the consumer.

Dynamic logistics companies realise that they can assume a competitively important responsibility by helping with the 'manufacturing' or the supply of 'after sales service', and they have therefore introduced what is called the 'value added logistics' concept. The VAL concept can be described as 'manufacturing in the pipeline'. Small interventions, often of a standardised nature (such as soldering on several modules, testing and packaging) are carried out by the logistics operators. Functions become intertwined, boundaries between sectors become blurred. Logistics help with the production and basic production is permeated with concepts such as 'value added logistics'.

→ *In value-added logistics, minor interventions, usually of a standardised nature, are carried out by logistics operators.*

102

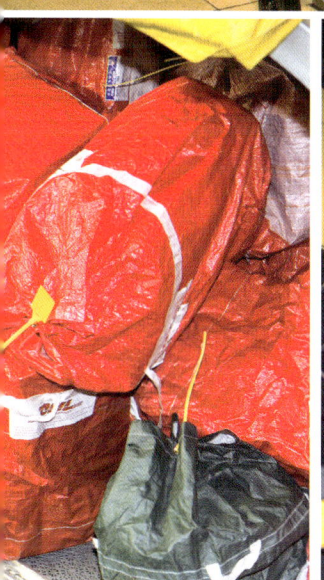

WAREHOUSES, MANAGING TIME, SPACE AND VALUE

Companies do not operate in a vacuum but in the market. What counts, more than ever before, is knowing and respecting the ground rules of the market. And this is not so easy. The information economy is changing drastically and with a spectacular speed the rules of the market.

Familiar and customary boundaries become blurred, new dimensions offer challenging possibilities and the customer is the unrelenting referee who determines who is successful and who is not. Companies must recognise the trends, keep an overview of the 'big picture', and keep pace with the needs of the customer.

No matter how accurately companies can adjust their 'supply chain' to the rules of the market, no matter how optimally the chain is orchestrated, logistic real estate remains an indispensable link in every network. More than ever, contemporary logistic real estate is designed to enhance the speed and the seamless connectivity of the logistic chain. It is a powerful instrument for actively and proactively responding to every trend on the market. It is the turbocharger of every logistic network. It determines the commercial policy of the company.

To convince yourself of the value of a warehouse in the logistic chain, consider briefly the value of your own private warehouse at home, your refrigerator. You buy food, you store that food in your refrigerator until you need it and you eventually take it to the place where you want to process or consume it. What is the value of your refrigerator? What is the value of having milk in the house at the moment that you want to use it? What does it cost not to have a refrigerator? Luke-warm milk, sour milk or no milk at all, a waste of time and expense, and inconvenience because you have to be continually running to the shops. Just like your refrigerator, a warehouse is the optimum storage place for products that might be needed at any time. It is a storage place that can save much time, much expense and much inconvenience.

Originally, warehouses mainly had a 'storage function'. For a 'push system', where production is based on the capacity (and thus not on demand), warehouses were indispensable buffers to take care of excesses in production. The more generic term 'warehouse' is now usually used for buildings in which storage (receiving, stocking, picking and shipping) is the most important function.

At present the production rhythm is being driven more and more by the demand of the consumer. The 'push system' is being replaced by a 'pull system' which reduces the need for pure storage. A contemporary warehouse has become more of a 'flow-through point' than a 'holding point'. It provides for faster delivery, better service, and to this end it continually generates real-time information about the stock and the flow of goods. Logistic buildings that are designed so the goods can be supplied to the consumer as fast and efficiently as possible, and because of this, perform all kinds of additional services (value-added activities), are called 'distribution centres' (DCs).

The logistic concept of a company has become a determining factor in the international competitive battle between companies. In some industries, costs related to logistics are less than 8% of the volume. In others the costs can be more than 40%. The price that the end user pays includes, on the average, 6% logistic costs[18].

Increasing liberalisation offers enormous new challenges and possibilities. National boundaries are continually losing more and more of their economic meaning, transport and communication are becoming cheaper and especially faster, national strategies are being replaced by multinational strategies, and both production and distribution are being reviewed, rationalised and optimised in a world-wide context.

Logistic real estate is playing an essential role in streamlining the logistic network. Logistic real estate has become a real discipline with real logistic estate-agent gurus or 'real estate professionals', who introduce new concepts and innovative strategies using the most impressive 'buzzwords'. In this case also, an update of the changes is immediately out-of-date (and thus incomplete) and any logical arrangement of the changes is impossible because they are often each others cause and effect. It is noticeable that these trends are also driven by forces such as connectivity, speed and optimisation of (immaterial) value. Consolidation, clustering, high-throughput facilities, cross-docking, flexibility, outsourcing, 'securitisation', and durable and aesthetically responsible construction are just a few examples of trends.

Consolidation

Because centralising or consolidating activities (related to both production and distribution) at the best possible location can yield important scale advantages, it follows that global provisioning, concentration of production and mass-customisation with postponed manufacturing (generic products are mass produced and are made customer-specific at the very end of the chain) are often part of the world-wide restructuring process. And this requires larger and more advanced warehouses. Smaller, national distribution centres are replaced by larger, higher (✱) distribution centres that deliver to customers in various countries.

Buildings with a few hundred-thousand square metres of surface area are no longer exceptions. With regard to the height, there is a clear evolution to higher buildings. According to construction technology you can of course make a building as high as you want. But the highest building is not the most optimal building economically. Taking the most diverse parameters into consideration, such as the price of the land, the height of the pallets, the speed at which pallets can be handled at higher positions, and the extra costs of a higher building, a free height (see infra) of more than 11 metres is seldom economically responsible.

This trend to 'bigger and better' is clearly illustrated by the rise of the consolidation centres. A consolidation centre is a large distribution centre, usually reserved for a very limited number, or even one category, of products. The idea is that the suppliers of those products, even though they are often each other's competitors, co-operate by storing their production in a common consolidation centre. A consolidation centre is often (not always) managed by one logistics service provider who takes care of the logistics of various, often competing, customers (✱).

The savings and optimisations that can be accomplished by such a logistic increase in scale are substantial: full loads both for incoming and outgoing transport, stock management by one administration, all kinds of scale advantages related to stock, storage and personnel costs.

* Schenker, one of the most progressive international logistics service providers, centralises products of its customers such as Nestlé, Douwe Egberts, Heinz, Oetker, Pab, General Biscuits and Delacre in the 52,000 m² large distribution centre at Kersdonk (realised by Eurinpro) on the logistic axis Antwerp-Brussels.

A22
A24
A26
A28
A30
A32
A34
A36
A38
A40
A42
A44
A46
A48
A50

CLUSTERING

Another strategy for making the deliveries fast and the costs efficient, is 'clustering'. Suppliers (often competitors) establish themselves in the immediate vicinity of manufacturers and form what are called 'manufacturing clusters'(✱).

Clustering is also used to bring products closer to the consumer so it is possible to respond to his wishes faster. This clustering, where finishing work is done in the vicinity of the point of sale, often occurs in the textile sector.

✱ Clustering is a trend that is especially common in the automobile industry. Ford's Chicago Manufacturing Campus consists of five buildings with a total surface area of 500,000 m² in which a dozen suppliers store their automobile parts. The Campus is located near the Ford assembly plant. According to estimates this rationalisation saves approximately 7.5 million litres of diesel per year[19].

HIGH-THROUGHPUT FACILITIES

For what are called 'time sensitive goods' such as high-technology goods, food stuffs or trendy goods, the speed of the logistic network is crucial. Each item that stays in the racks too long results in a loss. Large central distribution centres, located at a strategic location but not in the immediate vicinity of the consumer, are far from ideal. There is a need for small, fast, responsive, regional centres where one can obtain a very high degree of 'fulfilment'. Companies often have a hybrid network with, on the one hand, central distribution centres for their 'medium-turnover and slow-moving products' and, on the other hand, smaller regional distribution centres for the shipment of their 'fast-moving products'[20]. These distribution centres focus on a very fast rotation of goods and they operate around the clock. They are equipped with many loading and unloading docks, very advanced control equipment (✱), optimum order-picking systems (✱), and a well-planned warehouse lay-out.

* The control equipment and the warehouse trucks determine the dynamics in a warehouse.
To select the optimum control equipment, various factors are taken into consideration such as the storage methodology, the aisle width, the speed. At present, for example, much use is made of the 'rota-reach truck'. First, this truck only needs a 160 cm-wide passageway because the load can be set off sideways (so it is not necessary to turn in the aisle). This truck also has a high operational speed.
Contemporary trucks are often rail or induction guided (called Automatic Guided Vehicles or AGVs by insiders).

* The order-picking system (the way that orders are filled) is an important part of warehouse logistics. The labour factor and the associated labour costs play (along with, of course, the storage methodology) a major role in the choice of the right system. The introduction of new technologies in the warehouse drastically changes how, and how fast, orders can be processed.
'Pick by light', a technology based on Radio Frequency Identification, helps the worker find the location of the product quickly and accurately (because a light turns on above the product in question). At the same time the system processes all kinds of information such as the stock on hand and the order pattern ('pick by voice' is such a system).

CROSS-DOCKING

Delivery within 24 hours, e-commerce, telesales… Never before have the services of express companies been as highly valued as they are now. Although other companies also implement 'cross-docking' systems, they are mainly used by express services. Cross-docking has various, often complex, application modalities, but the main idea is that goods are not stored. Immediately on receipt they are prepared (usually only sorted) to be sent on to their final destination. Except for requiring many efficient loading and unloading docks (with preferably a big enough space to allow the trucks to manoeuvre easily) and a good organisation of the incoming and outgoing deliveries, cross-docking (usually) makes few demands on the warehouses (no optimum storage conditions are required; no advanced material handling systems are needed; simple, low 'big boxes', as they are called, are often sufficient). In countries where the climate allows it, cross-docking is sometimes done outside on parking lots near important traffic intersections.

Flexibility

Traditionally, the design of the building is adjusted to the flow of goods. On the basis of criteria such as turnover frequency, stock and storage volumes, incoming and outgoing volumes, and the specific characteristics of the goods, it is possible to determine the most suitable storage methodology (✱) and a building can be designed that is most suitable.

✱ **The storage methodology is the way the goods are stored in the building. In the design of a methodology one strives for a 'handling' (manipulation of goods) that is as efficient as possible. That efficiency relates both to the speed of processing and the occupancy of space in the warehouse (storage intensity). The pallet rack, for example, is one of the best known storage methods (storage of goods on pallets)**[21] .

Such a custom-designed warehouse will of course be most suitable for the anticipated activity, but it will seldom be the most valuable and durable building. The enormous changes in the market cause such warehouses to quickly become obsolete. Because of the continually shorter life-cycle and the strong growth in diversity of products, today's goods will no longer be the goods of tomorrow. The changing function (from storage to distribution) and the changing activities (value-added logistics) will quickly make that once so valuable 'warehouse' unsuitable and inefficient. Logistic real estate specialists succeed at realising multifunctional, and thus flexible, warehouses that will be valuable, not only today, but also in future (✱).

OUTSOURCING

The increasing tendency of integrally contracting out logistic real estate to a real estate specialist is another important driving force behind the demand for flexible immovable property. Companies – even logistics companies – concentrate on their core activities and decide to invest in them rather than in real estate. They replace the risk of a (large) long-term investment in immovable property with flexible short-term contracts (such as rental and leasing contracts) which enable them to easily take advantage of changing market conditions. It goes without saying that the professional investor cannot be tempted by a building that is adjusted for one possible user who in addition only wants to commit himself to a short-term rental formula. A valuable logistic building combines the actual desires of the user with the future-oriented requirements of the investor to become a 'state-of-the-art multifunctional' logistic building.

→ *International express firms deliver about two million international shipments each day.*

※ To distribute its goods in Europe, the Japanese company, Sony, centralised its logistic activities at two distribution centres. For the sales market in Belgium, Holland and Germany, Eurinpro realised a 120,000 m² distribution centre at Tilburg (Holland). The building can be divided into four equal blocks, each of which can be subdivided again by means of an extra diagonal separation, into eight smaller warehouses, each equipped with the necessary loading and unloading docks, office blocks, etc. Because of this flexible construction, parts of the building can be rented to third parties at times when less storage volume is needed.

Securitisation

Logistic real estate has become a separate profession with very specialised know-how. Because of the strategic and proactive approach of the 'real estate professional' this market has attracted the interest of institutional investors. 'State-of-the-art multifunctional' logistic immovable property, translated into moveable values, has now become a sought-after diversification in many investment portfolios (✱).

Durable

A demand for durable construction is common. The possibilities for meeting contemporary needs with durable or ecologically responsible materials, technologies and concepts, without limiting the possibilities of tomorrow, are virtually inexhaustible (✱).

The extra costs of a durable total concept are very high and for that reason it is seldom an economically responsible investment. The most durable building, both ecologically and economically, is usually the flexible polyvalent building with an undisputed long-term value (which, certainly in Western Europe, must comply with exacting environmental regulations).

✱ **According to the example of the American REITs (Real Estate Funds) Eurinpro launched the real estate investment company Siref on the Brussels stock exchange in 1999. The Siref portfolio consists of 18 logistic buildings in the Brussels-Antwerp region with a real estate value of about 110 million euros and a debt burden of only 25%.**

✱ **Gazeley (UK) profiles itself as a developer of durable logistic buildings. In Bedford, Gazeley developed a logistic platform with techniques such as solar energy, wind turbines, water recycling, combined with such things as the use of recyclable materials**[22].

Aesthetically responsible

Logistic buildings, often located on important main roads, are a perfect 'signboard' for the image of both the 'real estate specialist' and the users. Both are conscious of this, and increasingly, as time goes by, the grey monotony of the tin boxes is broken by striking aesthetic details or even architectural masterpieces.

138

LET THE MARKET IN...

The faster the market changes, the larger and thus more dangerous the gap between the internal organisation of the company and the market threatens to become. The best way to master the 'blur' is to let the market into your company. Focus on what happens outside the company, open the borders of the company, let the market guide the organisation. Embrace the creed 'the firm is never firm'[23].

With outsourcing of logistic real estate, what is called the 'state-of-the-art multifunctional warehouse' made its entry on the logistic real estate market. But companies now need more that an ingenious state-of-the-art warehouse that can be imitated and maybe even improved.

They want a personalised logistic 'total concept', the value of which greatly exceeds the material value of the building. Continually, the market for logistic real estate is becoming more specialised and more knowledge intensive, and co-operation among the various players is becoming more direct.

The vertically integrated company was the success model of the twentieth century. Doing everything yourself worked perfectly when information was scarce and markets were underdeveloped. Companies could rightly believe 1 + 1 = 3. But this model no longer works now when everyone can easily know what can best be bought where. The once so solid 'do everything yourself' company has, in the current information economy, become a many-headed monster that, not knowing which direction to look, is doomed to die out. Each part of the company, each activity, must be able to withstand the competitiveness test, the 'reality check' with the market. Does the (internal) price (and of course also the quality) of your own steel factory, legal department, bookkeeping, restaurant, logistics, housing meet the standards of the market? No? Why then do you continue to buy it from yourself? A non-competitive sideline weakens the competitive strength of the product or service that forms your 'core-business'. Better products and services can be obtained on the open market. It is time to welcome the market into your company, because the most efficient organiser of the company is the market, driven by the uncensored laws of supply and demand. Buy from the best and do yourself only what you do best. The new law has become 3 - 1 = 4.

This model is continually gaining in importance. Companies focus on knowing, doing and possessing things that are unique and world-class for a certain group of customers. This is what is called their 'customer value proposition'[24]. Only in this way are they able

to deal with the enormous changes in the market. They outsource all unavoidable peripheral activities to the best companies on the market. Companies are becoming flexible, dynamic structures, with each unit focusing all of its resources on its specific customer value proposition. It goes without saying that this model continually leads to more advanced, more specialised and more knowledge-intensive markets for products and/or services.

And this is exactly what has happened on the market for logistic real estate. Companies (also logistics companies) realise that an ability to adapt themselves to changing market conditions is essential for the success of their business. 'You cannot manipulate changes, you can only stay ahead of them[25].' And for this, flexibility is the watchword. Companies are searching for substantial flexibility. Owning their own logistic immovable property – a long-term investment, very capital intensive and by its nature immovable – decreases their flexibility on the changing, often uncertain and thus risky markets. The building asset, that once was valued so highly on the balance sheet, turns out to be a false god that can be better outsourced (also the ownership) to a specialist in that market. Logistic real estate professionals have re-conceptualised logistic real estate and have replaced the immobile, capital-draining and inflexible 'standard product' with an easily marketable, flexible 'custom solution'. In addition, with their very specific 'value proposition' they have launched a completely new business model on this market.

State-of-the-art logistic facilities

Outsourcing is the way to create flexibility, to keep pace with the market. Once outsourcing is introduced on a market, it is the merciless law of supply and demand that judges the quality of the products on that market. This is also true on the market for logistic real estate. The increasing outsourcing of logistic immovable property has resulted in a very fast and far-reaching professionalisation of the market.

Users of logistic real estate have become 'customers' and therefore also behave like customers. They are more demanding than ever before. They avoid long-term commitments but they still want the best building for their specific enterprise. It goes without saying that the logistic real estate professional can only invest in an (expensive) 'customised facility' if the concept of the building is multifunctional because that determines whether the building can be easily used for other, new activities and technologies and whether it is therefore a durable and consequently a valuable investment. Warehouses are no longer 'standardised boxes', sometimes derisively called 'cardboard boxes' or 'big boxes'. Valuable contemporary logistic buildings reconcile the long-term wishes of the investor with the short-term wishes of the user into a polyvalent 'state-of-the-art multifunctional facility'.

A 'state-of-the-art multifunctional facilities' must meet many, often exacting and/or complicated criteria. To give an idea of the complexity of the concept, a few of the most understandable criteria will be briefly explained.

General

Appearance is deceptive. From a technical viewpoint, warehouses are very simple constructions, but even the simplest implementation requires very specific knowledge. Consider, for example, how much water the roof surface of a warehouse of 50,000 m^2 has to be able to bear. Suppose that 0.05 litres of rain fall per second (which is not impossible), this means that a weight of 180 litres of water (180 kg) per m^2 and in total therefore a weight (distributed, of course) of no less than nine tons on the roof! A warehouse must therefore be equipped with an adequate rain drainage system. In each country there are standards that (on the basis of rain statistics) specify the capacities of the rain drainage system and thus determine, among other things the diameter of the drain pipes, the capacity of the gutter spouts in the roof (gutter spouts spout the water down from the roof and are extremely important if a drainage pipe becomes plugged up). This norm is only one of many – that can also be different in each country – the observance of which, and thus a perfect technical execution, is crucial for the safety of the building.

Strategic location

A warehouse in the middle of the desert, someplace near the North Pole or in the heart of a jungle, is worthless. Warehouses, and certain 'distribution centres', require a well-thought-out strategic location. Access to various traffic networks (road, rail, water, air) is important, and even essential for time-sensitive products. For these products, being in the immediate vicinity of an (extensive) sales market is also an indisputable advantage. Fast accessibility from a competitive labour market is an advantage that has especially become more important in recent years. To the extent that additional activities (which often are also more specialised) are carried out at the distribution centre, it must also be possible to find the right people to perform these tasks on acceptable conditions. New trends, such as cross-docking, clustering and consolidation, involve different and additional requirements related to the strategic location of the buildings. Only the logistic real estate professional knows which possibilities on the market are most suitable for the strategic concerns of the warehouse user.

→ *Access to various traffic networks defines the strategic location and therefore the value of logistic real estate.*

CONCEPT

The concept of the building must provide for an ideal warehouse arrangement that makes it possible for goods to be manipulated and stored as efficiently and optimally as possible; it must be possible to support supplemental activities (value-added activities); it must be possible for it to be easily adapted to quickly evolving communication infrastructure, control equipment, order-picking systems and the needs of new users; if it is a very large warehouse it must be easy for it to be subdivided into smaller warehouses for various users as required; it must have a sprinkler system, and all this must be done in an extremely tight economic context.

DOORS AND LOADING DOCKS

All goods are loaded and unloaded via the loading docks of the warehouse. The functionality of a logistic building is therefore also greatly determined by the right number of doors and loading docks (preferably with the ideal dimensions), equipped with the most adequate dock equipment (∗).

∗ When determining the number of doors and loading docks, one must, among other things take into consideration the manoeuvring space a lorry needs to reach the doors or the loading docks without having to use public roads. For each door a check must be made with regard to the turning circle that is available for a lorry that must unload.

5
www.dpd.net DPD

Depot 530
Depot 530
DEPOT 167
CC 6335

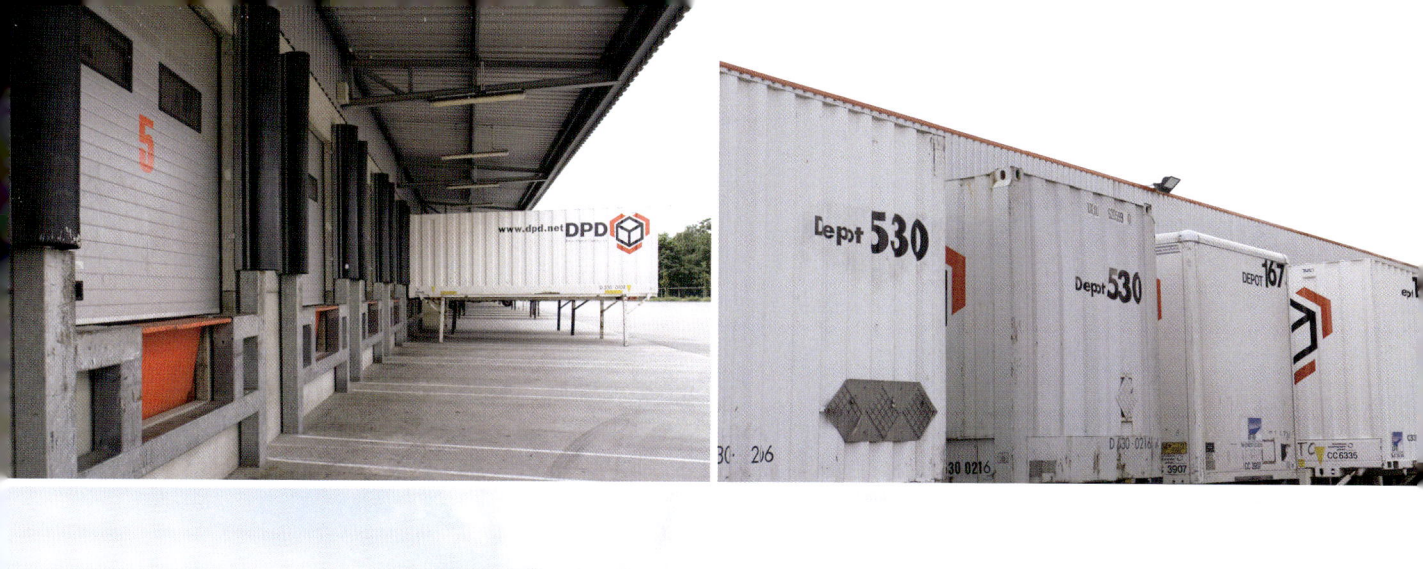

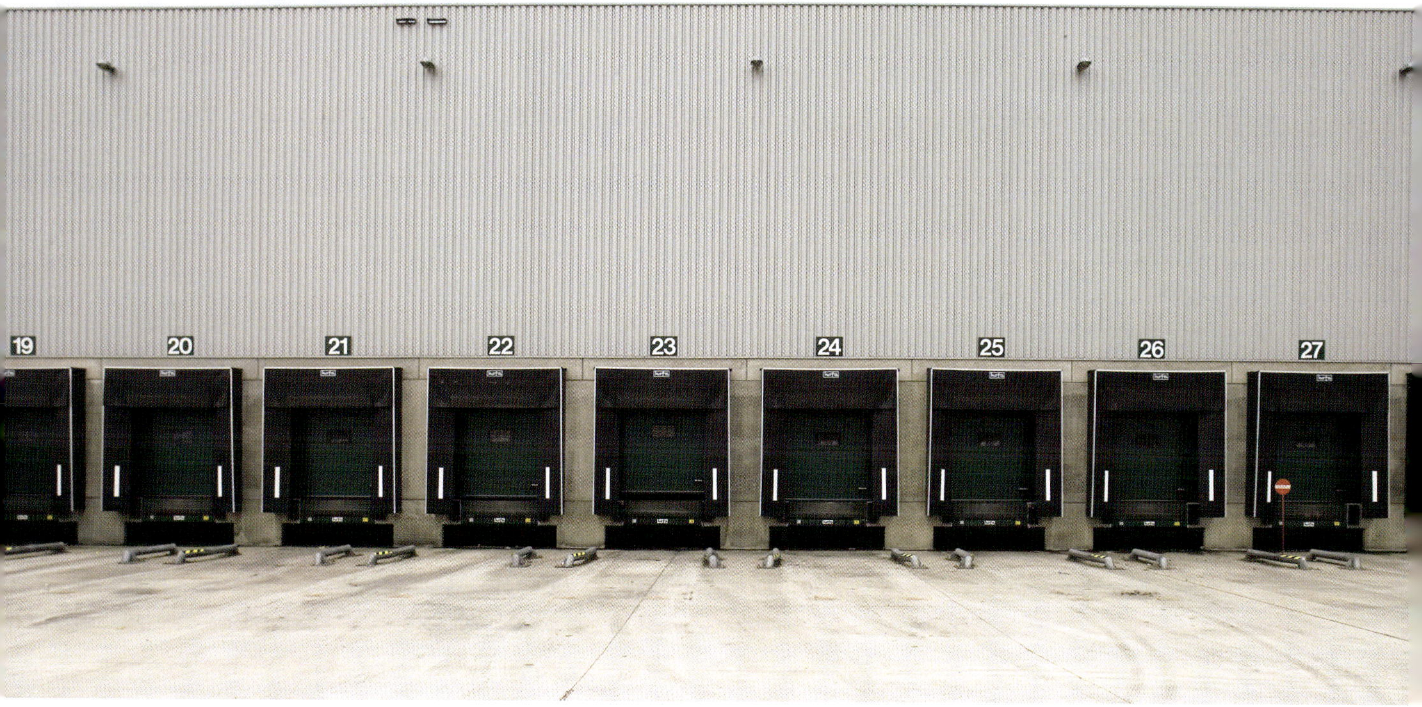
19
20
21
22
23
24
25
26
27

How the loading docks are finished off and equipped – such things as electric levellers, airbag docks, dock shelters and wheel guides… (✱) – has a big impact on the loading and unloading efficiency, and thus on the value of a building.

The free height of the building

The free height of the warehouse is the distance between the lowest point of the roofing structure and the floor of the building. Free height means capacity and is therefore just as important as surface area. The combination of various parameters such as the price of land, the height of the pallets or racks, the speed at which goods can be handled at higher positions, the extra costs of a higher building and the desired polyvalence, determines the optimum free height of a building.

✱ **'Levellers'** bridge the gap between the floor of the warehouse and that of the lorry. Dock-shelters ensure that during loading or unloading, the warehouse remains protected from the outside environment.

THE FREE SPAN OF THE BUILDING

The free span is the distance between two supporting columns of the building (✱).

✱ **In theory there are no limitations to the free span of structures. Consider, for example, the Golden Gate Bridge (San Francisco) of which the greatest span is 1280 metres or the Superdome (Louisiana) with its gigantic dome, which at once, thus without extra supports under the dome, spans an arena of 50,685 m².**

The installation of supports or columns in a warehouse always limits the subdivision possibilities and thus the flexibility of the building. The greater the span, the greater the storage capacity and the greater the free divisibility of the building becomes. Economically, it is nonsense, however, to design (super-expensive) warehouses without columns and which then would also have to be proportionally higher. The architectural optimisation of the span distances is a very technical calculation, which must take into consideration factors such as the height of the building, the choice of materials for the bearing structure (steel construction provides the greatest span), the dimensions of the pallets and the auxiliary equipment to be used. Taking all of these parameters into consideration, a free span of more than 36 metres seldom provides added value.

The floors

A carelessly floored warehouse is not useable. The floor of a warehouse must meet various criteria. The 'real estate specialist' takes care of the architectural optimisation of the floors, again on the basis of many different factors (including, of course, the influence of logistic systems on floor requirements).

\- - - the flatness of the floor:

The floor of a warehouse must be 'super-flat'. Especially in the aisles and certainly in high warehouses, the flatness must meet the highest criteria. Suppose that you are operating a forklift in the raised position and are manipulating a load of one ton at a set-off height of 10 metres. If the flatness of the floor would have a deviation of 1 cm in 1 m (which at a height of 10 m would result in a deviation of 10 cm) the truck would tilt and at a height of 10 metres you would hit the racks with the load. With such a deviation it would be impossible to place goods in the racks smoothly (or to take them out). For the sake of both the efficient handling of goods and the subdivision flexibility of the warehouse, the entire floor of a warehouse is almost always constructed super-flat (✱).

✱ **The** flatness of the floor is expertly verified. A deviation of 5 mm per 2 m (or a floor tolerance of 5 mm under a 2-metre long level) is not a problem for most warehouse users. The highest degree of flatness can be accomplished with a sub-floor on which a floor surface is applied (layers of epoxy, for example).

- - - the bearing power of the floors:

The floors of warehouses must be able to bear heavy loads (✱).

The higher a building is, the greater the bearing power of the floors must be. The desired bearing power of the floor is expressed in the number of kilograms that can be placed on the floor per m². A floor that can bear a uniform load of 5000 kg/m² (this is the weight of about five automobiles on one m²) has a high-grade bearing power.

In addition to various criteria related to bearing power, the compressive strength (also called the sustainable point pressure load) of the floor is also very important. It is quite possible for a floor to have sufficient bearing power for a distributed load that will cause no cracks or tears, but that the floor will be damaged at a place where the racks, loaded with tons of goods, rest on the floor. A floor that can stand a point pressure load of 25 kg/cm² without difficulty can be considered to be compression resistant.

✱ **The** bearing power of the floor may be ever so great, if the foundation of the warehouse has not been constructed to bear the same load, the floor will be worthless. The bearing power begins with the foundation of the building.

\- - - large monolithic surfaces:

With the development of advanced warehouse techniques, concrete floors have gained greater significance (✱).

✱ Concrete floors have great bearing power. They can sustain a point pressure load of as much as 400 kg/cm^2 [26]. Because of this characteristic, a concrete floor is very suitable for higher buildings. The materials mixed with the cement, the type of cement used and the ratio of water and cement, all determine the specific characteristics (including quality and price) of a concrete floor.

Concrete floors are poured. During drying concrete shrinks, which can cause cracks to appear in the floor. For this reason, seams are included in the floor. A monolithic surface is a surface on which no seams or contraction joints appear. The essential seams and joints can be perfectly sealed over with a pressure bearing surface coating (often in synthetic resin) that increases the wear-resistance of the floor and also keeps the floor dust-free.

Fire safety

There is no absolute standard that defines the fire safety of a logistic building. Usually, local regulations, and to an even greater extent, insurance-company specifications, determine the requirements. The high budget spent on fire safety, in exceptional cases being as much as 20% of the total construction cost, is a clear indicator of the importance of this aspect of the building.

The fire behaviour of the bearing structure, and of course also the building's use and thus its contents, greatly determine the fire safety of a building (✱).

The value of a building is partially determined by the presence of fire-security measures such as fire walls, advanced sprinkler installations (ESFR sprinklers), smoke detection, water screens, smoke evacuation hatches, smoke screens, and of course, sufficient fire hoses and hydrants.

Logistics and real estate, two powerful economic forces, have been interwoven into one 'core competence'. Only warehouses of which all parameters have been co-ordinated with great logistical and technical expertise, are worth investing in, and deserve a lasting place on the market.

✱ **Steel** has a very limited fire resistance of about fifteen minutes, on the average. This can be increased somewhat by applying some kind of 'coating' to the steel. A concrete bearing structure has good fire resistance and will support the building at least one hour (and possibly even two). The big problem (certainly for concrete, but also for steel) is unpredictability. For the firemen who come to put out the fire it is very difficult to estimate when the bearing structure will collapse. Concrete explodes, which causes the building to collapse suddenly. A heated steel structure will bend and then collapse.

With wood this is different. In a raging fire, a wooden beam will have burned in about 6 cm after an hour. Because the condition of the wooden structure can also be seen visually, the behaviour of the structure is much more predictable.

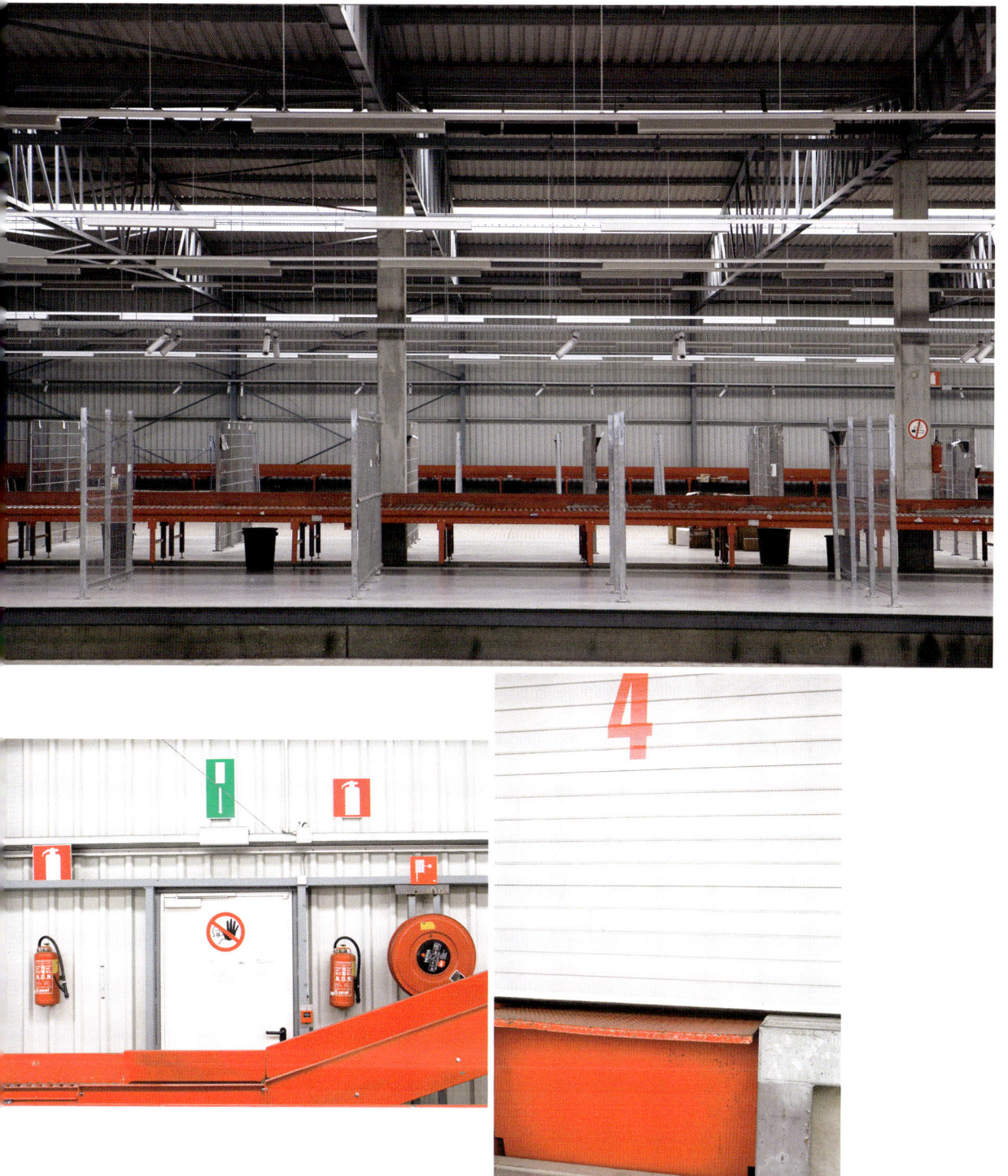

The value proposition of the logistic real estate specialist

Companies optimise their logistic chain and thus generate competitive advantage. This is not done a little at a time. A new market environment forces them (very often) to completely revise their supply chain, including, of course, their real estate. Thus, starting over from scratch is often the best alternative. It is not sufficient to have an ideal building that only gives them a temporary competitive advantage. They want a custom-designed logistic 'total concept' that provides them with an inimitable advantage, the value of which far exceeds the material value of the logistic building.

'Build a box, lease it, keep it or sell it, then move on to the next opportunity' (as the business of the developer has sometimes been described) is not the way the new real estate specialist works. The real estate specialist himself invests in the warehouse that he recommends. This prevents him from being transaction-driven. He himself bears the consequences (and thus risks) of his own advice. The concept that he presents to his customer must not only convince his customer but must also be attractive for institutional investors to whom he offers his real estate as a financial product. And investors want qualitative investments with a good and certain long-term yield.

The new real estate specialists are relation builders. Their market is located at the crossroads of real estate, logistics, and the financial investment market for logistic real estate. In this specific market niche they are experts, and they control all aspects, so they can eliminate every imperfection. They want loyal customers, subcontractors who are proud to work with them, advisors who will go to the limit to find something better, institutional investors who are waiting for their financial product. Like a spider, the real estate specialist co-ordinates his web of relations. His web is woven with loyalty and is based on trust. He must earn this trust and loyalty with his reputation. And this assumes that he knows his profession better than anyone else. You can only choose your relations correctly, however, if you have sufficient knowledge in house (and this is just as important) to evaluate them properly. The 'value proposition' of the real estate specialist can be summarised as follows[27].

165

• **The package of services offered by the real estate specialist includes 'all-in' costs** (such as rent, maintenance, fiscal fees and costs, and the management of the building). For the customer, this means a clear, well-defined budget.

• **The real estate specialist is a 'one-stop shop'** and has therefore a very flexible package of services. A solution is found wherever a solution is needed (✱).

The real estate specialist also makes good use, for example, of the trend toward more regional (and thus smaller) strategically located distribution centres. They can easily offer these smaller warehouses in addition to a large distribution centre. These 'multi-tenant warehouses' are very attractive (also with regard to price) because of the scale advantages that can be accomplished.

Only a very limited number of real estate specialists can handle the challenging, exacting demands of contemporary clients. This presupposes an expert multidisciplinary team of employees who, in spite of the focus on their own discipline in the logistic real estate niche, also have the expertise required to maintain a panoramic view of each concept and to evaluate it critically in its entirety.

✱ **JVC** had a storage space of 4000 m2 at Roissy (France). For various reasons this distribution centre was no longer satisfactory. In addition, JVC preferred to get rid of the investment burden rather than to keep it. Eurinpro proposed a total solution in which they purchased the existing warehouse of JVC by means of a swap operation, together with an adjoining piece of land of 5000 m². After Eurinpro renovated, adapted and expanded the obsolete warehouse, it was rented to Computacenter. Eurinpro bought a piece of land for JVC in Carrières-sur-Seine (near the airport) on which they built a completely new European distribution centre of 10,000 m² with 4000 m² of offices.

A 'SIMPLY BETTER' FUTURE

The current supply of products is unbelievably great. Virtually anything we can imagine is for sale. The supermarket presents us with a wealth of products. Our chairs, offices, kitchens and houses are more comfortable than our parents could have imagined. Special trips, sensational holidays, can simply be booked and experienced. We are surrounded by multifarious forms of comfort, wealth, and even super-abundance. Yet we often have the feeling that something is lacking.

Swamped with information about products that are often not even of interest to us, it becomes increasingly difficult to find precisely the right product. And then, once found, it is often unavailable. It appears that we are most frustrated by an absence of reliable service after we have purchased the product. Consumers no longer dream about having more, different or sensational products, they just want better products.

Real consumer-oriented innovation is less common than we might expect. Inventing the wheel again, but this time square because it is new and exciting, has no value whatever. It would only be confusing and annoying. The really valuable innovation or technology is one that succeeds at giving the consumer exactly what he wants. Not only the consumers we already know about, but all six billion fellow human beings on our earth, now and in the future.

There is still much room for valuable technological innovation and economic growth.

Has the consumer really become 'king'? It cannot be denied that the changes have been immense. The (super)abundance of products and information provides us with every imaginable (and even unimaginable) form of comfort. With regard to choices, our lives are richer than our grandparents could have ever dreamed. But is consuming really such a feast? And, can companies really claim to be 'consumer-centric[28]'? In the consumption process, three times can be observed when the consumer's expectations are often disappointed:

• **We increasingly spend more time and energy on our search for the right product.** The explosion of possibilities causes us to surf for hours on the web. Is this the right product? Where is the closest distributor? Does he offer the product for the right price? Without even knowing it, we do a large part of the work of the seller. We fill in forms with our preferences, submit orders ourselves, install software so we can make payments ourselves and we even follow the progress of our order on the Internet. This of course makes it easy for the seller, but do we actually want to do all these things? Do we want to spend our time on this? Time that we continually have less of and which is therefore increasingly valuable. In an age of double-income couples, single parents and a (less energetic) greying population, the effort required to consume actually ought to decrease.

→ *We use goods our grandparents could not have even imagined.*

• ***Are the goods that we want really within our reach?*** Is the right product really available, precisely at the moment that we need it? The overcrowded shelves of shops might cause one to think that it is. Yet, this can be deceiving. In the average grocery shop you can find, on the average, (only) 92% of the products on the shelves[29]. Since the customer, on the average, has 40 items on his shopping list, this means that he can buy all the items he needs in one shop only one time out of twenty. Thus nineteen times out of twenty, he will have to buy something else, go to a different shop, or change his plans somewhat. In short, the right product is not available where and when he wants it.

• ***But even if we find the right product at the right moment, at the right place, then the question still remains whether our 'consumption problem' will actually be solved.*** Take the purchase of a new computer, for example. It has to be installed and of course preferably integrated with our other (electronic) equipment. Do we really have the right software, cables and network access? Who will take care of the maintenance, repairs, upgrading and finally the recycling of the materials? This process seldom goes smoothly. Help lines, waiting times, always someone else (who does not seem to be listening) to whom we must explain our problem for the umpteenth time. We simply want everything to operate dependably, to connect seamlessly, without a waste of time, without stress, without frustration. And that is certainly not always the case.

For years it was believed that you could only win (and keep) the consumer by giving him something new, something different, something that no one else had ever thought of before. Innovations were made, revolutionary thinking was used, rules were superseded, boundaries were moved, because the motto was 'differentiate or die'. But while frantic work was being done to develop new bells and whistles, a large number of consumers were waiting 'on hold'. They were waiting for the right information about the right product, for the product that is always available when and where they want it, for a product with integrated service. They preferred something reliable to something completely new. Thus, innovation and differentiation are not a striving for sensation and excitement, but simply for doing it better, 'simply better'[30], giving exactly what is requested. The rest is ballast, superfluous waste.

Here lies an enormous challenge and opportunity for production, sellers, the service sector and logistics providers. Put yourself in the place of the consumer. How can the consumption process be optimised, streamlined, stripped of everything the consumer does not request or want? This is the chalk mark for improving your offer. This is the basic idea of a completely new movement – even with its own school – namely 'lean consumption'. It is the movement that perfectly complements the just-in-time principle (that concentrates on the production side). Make an effort to discover what the consumer really wants. The rest is superfluous.

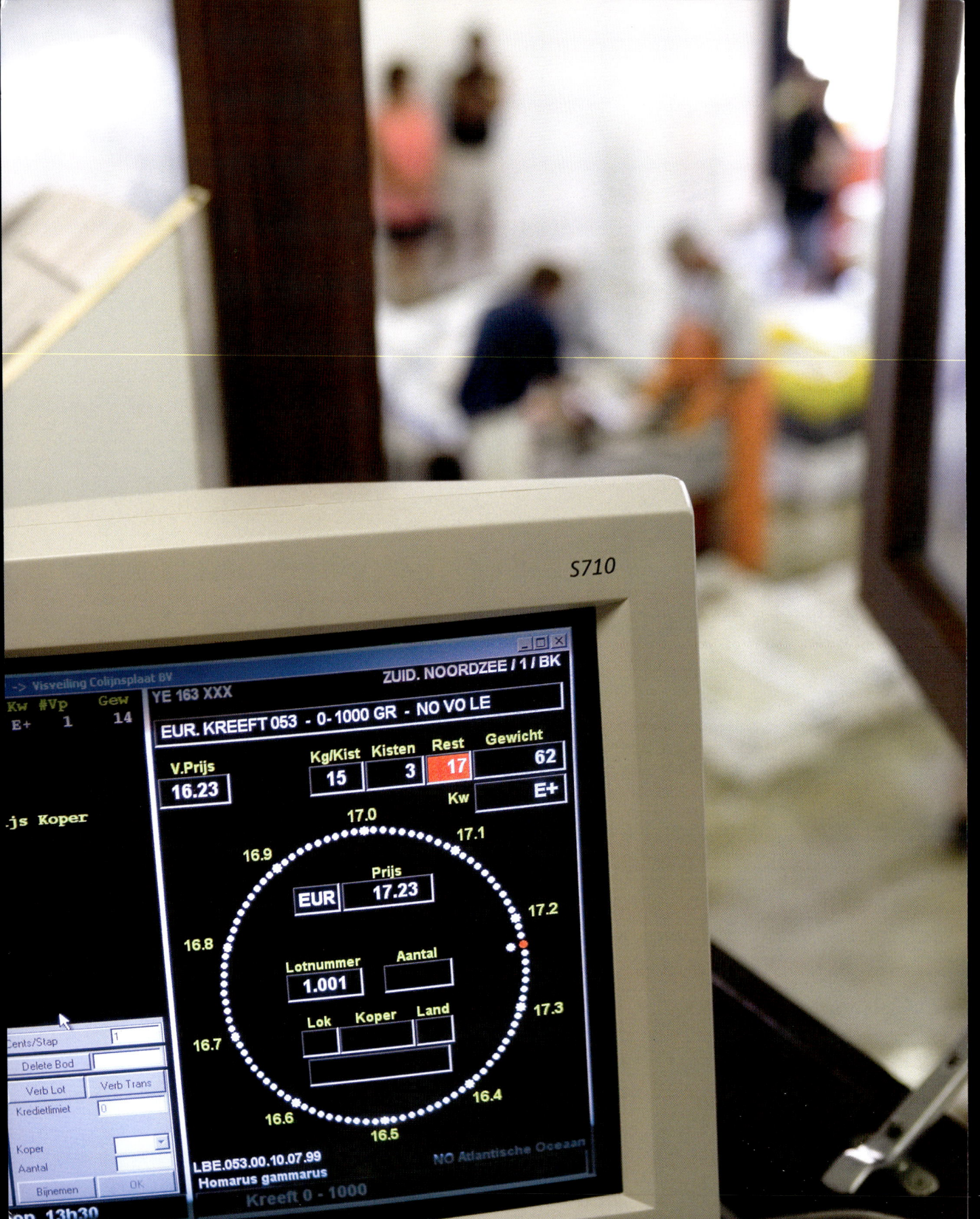

Edmund's interactive website is a complete information source for the buyer of a new or used car. Edmund consulted a team of psychologists specialised in consumer behaviour, who designed a website that would satisfy the wishes of the customers as closely as possible. The site won various awards, not because of a 'flashy design' and 'colourful pop-ups', but because of the simplicity, the user friendliness, and what is called the 'customisation' of the site.

In three years time Daewoo Motors gained one percent market share on the difficult British market. They succeeded at this by asking automobile users what they really hate about the use or purchase of an automobile. On the basis of this information Daewoo was able to put together a market-conquering service package. Daewoo sells ordinary cars but in a (unique) way that gives the consumer what he likes.

The market for logistic real estate also has a representative of this basic idea. What Eurinpro offers is and remains a warehouse, one which certainly deserves the description 'state-of-the-art'. Yet, with their know-how they have been able to take the immobile, capital-draining and inflexible (standard) product and make it into a flexible custom solution, complete with integrated service, exactly tuned to the wishes and needs of their customers[31].

In future, the customer will probably become even more the 'king'[32]. The whole chain will make the consumer the focal point of everything, also at the very front of the chain. Even suppliers of raw materials will focus on the wishes of the customer. And this assumes, of course, that we know and understand the wishes of the customer, that we can individualise customer requirements. And for this, the co-operation of the customer is needed (and indeed that of everyone in the chain) but it may not cost him much time and effort.

This is not an unrealistic challenge now that everything around us is becoming 'smart' and continually 'smarter'. Our sport shoes keep track of how many kilometres we run, our chair remembers how we like to sit, our grill knows exactly whether we want our meat 'well done' or still a little red in the middle. Products that we buy are increasingly provided with small processors and memories. At present they usually concentrate on their own task, they only talk to themselves.

Soon, however, they will be connected with each other, they will integrate their activities and data, they will be interactive and will work together. Without it requiring any effort on the part of the customer, data can be 'captured'. From this data, information can be produced, and the supply, and even the whole logistic chain, can be adjusted to the demand. Take the simple example of Coca-Cola soft-drink machines. In Japan there are more than 800,000 of them, all provided with a chip. What does such a soft-drink machine need to know? How many cans are left? How often was the button pressed of a drink that was no longer available? When and where are the most/least sold? Does the customer want large cans or preferably a smaller size? If all these machines are connected, become part of a network, then you have a powerful interactive system that provides you with the knowledge you need to better supply an unmodified basic product (in this case soft drink) and also to avoid excessive costs.

If the focus is on the consumer during the whole life-cycle of a product (and thus not only at the end), logistics will become an even broader and more complex concept. The services that companies offer will encompass the whole life-cycle of the product, and will possibly become even more important that the (ownership of the) product itself. We often want products because of their usefulness, possibly their symbolic value, but we do not necessarily care whether we own them or not. Consider the automobile, for example, which is often rented or leased. Would it not be nice if our carpet were regularly taken away and replaced with a new one in the latest colours? We replace our television and camera after a time with one that is better and nicer. How often can we wear that expensive designer dress? How often do we buy the use of a product when we are not at all concerned about possessing it?

If this is true, 'reverse logistics' is given a new meaning. Reverse logistics (currently just the collection of entirely or partially used goods in the framework of recycling logistics) will then form an integral part of distribution logistics because when goods become services, the logistic chain only stops when the product returns to the seller or even to the manufacturer. The logistic chain would become even longer and even more complicated.

But how can that be a problem in a world in which technology evolves continually faster? When objects can be connected with each to form a 'smart system', when maybe even the human brain can be part of a network, it should be possible to create extremely efficient IT-driven logistic systems. Nanotechnology might also make our products lighter, stronger, cheaper and more environmentally friendly, and might allow production to occur much faster. Only then would just-in-time really be just-in-time. Even the speed and efficiency with which goods are moved (which now often costs the most time and difficulty) are steadily increasing. With 'Fastship' cargo, all goods will soon be able to cross the ocean in record time (and much cheaper)[33]. By means of completely computer controlled 'tube freight technology' (known as capsules in pipelines) goods can be pumped to their destination underground without delays caused by weather, traffic jams or accidents.

As that may be, companies will continue to optimise their logistic chain. To the extent that they can better analyse their 'core strengths' they will be able to outsource even more tasks and organise themselves even more efficiently, and all of this for King Customer.

And what does the customer think about it?
Around the turn of the century approximately one and a half billion of the six billion people were part of the consumer class. They can meet their basic needs and also afford some luxury as well. The logistic chain leads mainly (and almost exclusively) to these consumers. As many as three billion people live in fast-developing economies and are ready to join this class. China and India, the two most densely populated countries in the world, are industrialising at top speed. They represent a billion and a half people who do not (yet) belong to the consumer society.

An enormous number of people are anxious to become part of the consuming class, to own a radio, a refrigerator, a television, an automobile, a computer. But will there be enough raw materials and clean air to enable all people to participate in our consumption? If in time the third world also lays claim to the same level of affluence, our planet will go irreversibly to its ruin, is what many ecological scarcity worriers are thinking. And according to them, this is reason enough to consume less. Karim Benammar thinks this is just doom-mongering. Consuming less only postpones the problem. Rather than destroying the world in fifty years, we will do it in a hundred years. Stopping economic growth means condemning the underprivileged to enduring poverty world-wide. What right does the rich West have to deny people in the third world the possession of a refrigerator, mobile phone, computer, or automobile when they have two or three?

The real problem is not the depletion of raw materials and energy but that we still operate our production on the basis of non-replaceable raw materials and energy. Scarcity is the proof of our lack of creativity. As soon as science finds a solution for this, our earth will be able to successfully support six billion people with the same standard of living as ours[34].

Footnotes

(1) Handy, C., Why companies may be held to ransom by their employees, UBF, 2001 a

(2) Business week, 28 August 2000

(3) Euro RSCG

(4) Saatchi&Saatchi

(5) Karaokekapitalisme, Kjell A. Nordström and Jonas Ridderstrale, Lannoo, 2003

(6) De parende geest

(7) Sherry Turkle, 'The fellow of the microchip', Globalisation, 2004

(8) Karaokekapitalisme, pg 144

(9) Stan Davis, Lessons from the future, 2001

(10) Karaokekapitalisme, pg 146

(11) Karaokekapitalisme, pg 227

(12) Mastering the challenges of the supply chain, 2003, pg 116

(13) Business Logistics, '3PL is goed, 4PL is beter', November 2004

(14) Mastering the challenges of the supply chain, 2003, pg 30

(15) Dr R. Lieb, The use of 3PL services by large American manufacturers, September 2004

(16) Mastering the challenges of the supply chain, 2003, pg 112

(17) Logistiek, laatste front in de concurrentieslag, 26th Vlaams Wetenschappelijk Congres, March 2004, pg 131

(18) Just-in-time real estate, Anne B. Frej, ULI, 2004, pg 17

(19) Exceptional Industrial Projects, NOIP, 2003, pg 10

(20) Mastering the challenge of the supply chain, pg 81

(21) Operationele interne logistiek, Gerben Esmeijer, Academic Service, 2001

(22) www.gazeley.co.uk

(23) Stan Davis, Lessons from the future, 2001, pg 137

(24) Nordström e.a., Karaokekapitalisme, pg 224

(25) Peter Drucker, 1999

(26) Gerben Esmeyer, Operationele interne logistiek, 2001, pg 183 ff

(27) Mastering the challenges of the supply chain, Roland Berger, 2003, pg 71

(28) Power at last, The economist, April 2005

(29) Lean consumption, J.P Womack and D. T. Jones, Harvard Business Review, March 2005

(30) Simply better, Winning and keeping customers by delivering what matters most, P. Barwise and S. Meehan, Harvard Business Shool, August 2004

(31) De value chain als wissel op de toekomst, W. Ploos van Amstel, Business Logistics, April 2005

(32) www.eurinpro.com

(33) Just-in-time real estate, A. Frej, ULI, 2004, pg 25 ff

(34) Overvloed, Karim Benammar, Veen magazines, 2005

Index

Aisle	121, 156
Alliances	84
Arch consumer	68
Bearing power	158
Bearing structure	163
Blur	95, 80
Business webs	84
Cellae	38
Centralisation	88
Clustering	118
Compressive strength	158
Consolidation	112
Consolidation centre	114
Consumer-centric	174
Consuming less	186
Contract logistics	91
Contraction joint	160
Core competence	84
Core strengths	144
Cross-docking	124
Customer value proposition	144
Customised	98
Distribution centre	108
Dock equipment	150
Dockshelters	154
Docks	44
Epoxy	156
Expedition	88
Express company	96
Fast response	62
Fastship	184
Fire resistance	163
Flex-buildings	21, 128
Floor tolerance	156
Free height	115
Free span	155
Fulfilment	18, 120
Globalisation	58
Holding point	108
Horrea	38
Impulse buying	60
Inbound transport	88
Induction guided	121
Information economy	82, 86
Integrator	96
JIT	16
Kanban System	16
Lean consumption	20, 178
Levellers	154
Loading docks	150
Logistic chain	14
Logistic platforms	33
Logistic solution	21
Love brand	60

Manufacturing clusters	118	Reliability	96
Mass consumer	20	Resources	87
Mass customisation	98	Reverse logistics	184
Material handling system	124	Securitisation	132
Monolithic surface	160	Smart shopper	58
Multi-tenant warehouses	168	Smart system	184
Network arrangers	86, 90	State-of-the-art multifunctional logistic building	146
Off-balance constructions	166	Storage intensity	126
One party logistics - 1PL	88	Storage methodology	121
One-stop shopping principle	90	Super responsive	64
One-stop shop	168	Super-flat	156
Order-picking system	121	Supply chain	14
Outbound transport	88	Synergy	88
Outsourcing	88, 128, 143	Tags	92
Pallet rack	126	Third party logistics – 3PL	90
Pass-through centre	21	Time sensitive goods	120
Pick by light	121	Tube freight technology	184
Point pressure load	158	Turnover frequency	126
Postponed manufacturing	98	Two party logistics – 2PL	88
Prosumer	60	Value added logistics	98
Pull system	108	Value-chain	80
Pull economy	58, 108	Vertical integration	84
Radio Frequency Identification	92	Virtual network	78
Rail guided	121	Warehouse truck	121
Rain drainage system	148	Wheel guides	121
Relation builder	164		
Real estate professional	164		
Real time	82		

www.lannoo.com

Lannoo Publishers

Kasteelstraat 97

8700 Tielt

Belgium

lannoo@lannoo.be

TEXT Ann De Kelver

PHOTOGRAPHY Koen Van Damme (with the exception of p. 166-167)

LAYOUT Inge Van Damme

PRINTED AND BOUND BY Drukkerij Lannoo, Tielt

© Lannoo Publishers, Tielt, 2006

D/2005/45/380 • ISBN 90 209 6240 X • NUR 450-454

All rights reserved. No part of this book may be reproduced, stored in a retrieval system,

or transmitted in any form or by any means, electronic, electrostatic, magnetic tape,

mechanical, photocopying, recording or otherwise, without the prior permission in

writing of the publisher.